MAINTAINING INDUSTRIAL DISCIPLINE

MAINTAINING INDUSTRIAL DISCIPLINE

Answers to 50 Frequently Asked Questions

G.P. DAS GUPTA

Los Angeles I London I New Delhi
Singapore I Washington DC I Melbourne

First published in 2002 by

SAGE Publications India Pvt Ltd
B1/I-1 Mohan Cooperative Industrial Area
Mathura Road, New Delhi 110 044, India
www.sagepub.in

SAGE Publications Inc
2455 Teller Road
Thousand Oaks, California 91320, USA

SAGE Publications Ltd
1 Oliver's Yard, 55 City Road
London EC1Y 1SP, United Kingdom

SAGE Publications Asia-Pacific Pte Ltd
3 Church Street
#10-04 Samsung Hub
Singapore 049483

Published by Vivek Mehra for SAGE Publications India Pvt Ltd, typeset in 11pt Sanskrit-Palatino by S.R. Enterprises, New Delhi, and printed at Chaman Enterprises, New Delhi.

Library of Congress Cataloging-in-Publication Data

Das Gupta, G.P., 1939-
 Maintaining industrial discipline: answers to 50 FAQs/G.P. Das Gupta.
  p. cm.
 Includes bibliographical references and index.
 1. Labor discipline. I. Title.

HF5549.5.L3 D37 2002   658.3'14–dc21   2001058125

ISBN: 978-93-515-0912-7 (PB)

The SAGE Team: Leela Gupta, Sushanta Gayen and Santosh Rawat

Contents

Foreword

The first edition of this book, titled *Industrial Discipline—Concepts, the Law and Cases* was published a decade ago. This revised edition incorporates the sea changes which have taken place in industrial relations since then, and will be an invaluable and practical guide to those who have to deal regularly with the subject at ground level.

Mahatma Gandhi was an acknowledged champion of the poor and disadvantaged sections of society. His 'Ahmedabad Experiment' dealt with the problems of industrial workers whom he described as 'sweated labour'. It gave him a deep insight into the exploitation of industrial workers in the textile industry. As a result of this experiment, the leaders of the Swaraj movement were convinced that a fundamental change in the social order was necessary. Accordingly, two important declarations of far-reaching importance were made in Article 38 of the newly framed Indian Constitution. These declarations underlined that the state 'shall strive to promote the welfare of the people by securing and protecting, as effectively as it may, a social order, in which justice, social, economic and political shall guide, all the institutions of the national life'. The state was directed to further strive to minimize the inequalities in income, and endeavour to eliminate inequalities in status, facilities and opportunities not only amongst individuals, but also amongst groups of people residing in different areas or engaged in different vocations. Towards this end, the

Directive Principles of State Policy were enunciated in Part IV of the Constitution. Under these Directives, the state was to provide humane conditions of work, fair wages, social security in old age, maternity benefits, etc. In order to implement these directives, between 1946 to 1990, numerous labour laws were enacted by the Parliament and state legislatures. The state by setting up public sector undertakings, discharged its obligation of creating a social order free from exploitation of employees in the public sector, compelling the private sector to emulate the same. However, while interpreting the provisions of labour laws, courts tended to favour the working class. Today, even in matters involving serious acts of indiscipline, the employer is severely constrained to justify the punishment meted out to a delinquent worker, notwithstanding the fact that an elaborate inquiry was held into the charges. In the process, employers have found it difficult to maintain discipline because of the excessive legal and judicial protection given to workers. In recent times, there have been decisions galore from various judicial bodies, reversing administrative decisions in discharge and dismissal cases.

Institutions are manned by human beings who have their own predilections which guide them while accomplishing their goals. The judiciary is no exception and is also not free from prejudices. Otherwise how can one appreciate that the decision of the seven judges' bench in the Bangalore Water Supply and Sewerage Board vs Rajappa (1978 2 SCC 213), was questioned by a division bench fifteen years after it was delivered and consistently affirmed by dozens of judges.

The author's work deserves appreciation. His rich experience in an industrial organization of repute as well as his knowledge of the subject enabled him to highlight the pitfalls which managers face or are likely to face in maintaining discipline. He suggests several measures to tackle the problems in addition to bringing to the notice of Indian managers the ground level reality on the subject as it exists today. The vacillation of the judiciary in interpreting labour laws has been clearly brought out. The author has sincerely tried to bring out all the latest judgements and interpretations in this book, which I am sure will be of great value to the reader. I wish it every success.

Justice D.A. Desai
Former Judge, Supreme Court of India
Former Chairman, Law Commission of India

Surat
18th March, 2001

Preface

It is well known that labour in India enjoys statutory, judicial and constitutional protection against unfair treatment by the employer. It is sometimes debated whether the right to life under Article 21 of the Constitution includes the right to continued employment under an employer. In some recent decisions, the Supreme Court of India has given new direction as to what constitutes a 'reasonable opportunity to defend' in a disciplinary enquiry. From time to time, the apex court has pronounced its verdict on what constitutes misconduct for which a worker can be punished, the rights of the employer to terminate the services of any employee, the constitutional rights of government employees and those employed in public sector enterprises, the validity of several rules and regulations relating to discipline and conduct of employees in public sector enterprises, the concept of natural justice and other related issues. In some cases, even old rules and regulations, a valid contract of employment, or provisions in the certified standing orders have been declared invalid. Today, no employer can terminate the services of a worker even for a bona fide reason like loss of confidence. Employers can better appreciate their role if they are not only aware but also receptive to the changing requirements of the society and the law. This book may serve as a useful reference on the subject to professional managers, trade union leaders and labour lawyers alike.

This book deals with the management of industrial discipline in all its ramifications including the latest case laws on the subject. Based on my professional experience of nearly four decades and interaction with practising managers in various management development programmes, the answers to 50 most frequently asked questions on the subject were framed and are duly supported by the relevant case laws.

I am extremely grateful to Justice D.A. Desai, former judge of the Supreme Court of India and former Chairman, Law Commission of India, who inspite of other commitments kindly scrutinized the manuscript and offered his valuable comments to enrich its contents. I am greatly honoured by his Foreword to the book.

Despite all my efforts to incorporate the latest case laws on each topic, there might be omissions on some score. I shall, therefore, be grateful to receive suggestions or comments from readers for improvement in this regard.

Jamshedpur   **G.P. Das Gupta**

ONE

Introduction

The word 'discipline' has been derived from the word 'disciple'. It implies obedience to a code of conduct supporting the ideologies and values of the time and an unqualified acceptance of authority. In the context of industry, it refers to conformity to the rules and procedures of the organization, the acceptance of the authority of superiors and the willingness to work for the objectives of the organization. The old master and slave relationship was gradually transformed into a master and servant or contractual relationship. In the course of time, with the development of human civilization and the emergence of concepts such as justice, equity and fairness the employer–employee relationship is the more relevant connotation where employees' interests are protected by a number of labour legislations based on social conscience and need of the time.

The maintenance of industrial discipline is a challenging problem of our times. Employees and their trade unions in the organized sector, whether in industrial establishments or educational institutions, offices or hospitals, periodically disrupt production and services. The ensuing breakdown of essential services like power generation and medical care in hospitals as a result of these disruptions creates unnecessary hardship to the public at large.

It is rather naive to presume that industrial establishments will remain totally unaffected by the general lack of discipline in our society. The enforcement of discipline in industry, is therefore a bigger challenge than we can imagine. The workforce today is better informed and is by and large, organized on political lines. It is therefore, not only their skill, professional competence or educational background, but also their political affiliation that more often determines their attitude towards the management's efforts either to increase production, improve productivity, quality or service or maintain industrial discipline. The protective laws that apply to these organized workers is to a large extent responsible for the lazy and contemptuous attitude towards the management. Various provisions under the Industrial Disputes Act, 1947 (IDA or the Act), relating to industrial harmony and the prevention and settlement of industrial disputes have quite often been violated. Despite statutory restrictions, strikes and lockouts continue to account for over twenty million mandays lost annually. Both the employers as well as the trade unions accuse each other for this malaise. While the employers feel that the militant attitude of the workers and multiplicity of trade unions coupled with job security are the main reasons for indiscipline, the trade unions attribute it to the conditions created by the management.

Apart from organized strikes in industries, there have been *gheraos*, wrongful restraint, use of force and threat to life and property. However, the law enforcement authorities usually step in only after the *gherao* is lifted, or when a search warrant has been issued. Apart from this, situations such as a go slow, work to rule (rule as the workers perceive it) and sympathetic strikes even where the workers' interests are not directly involved, are also common.

This malady has pervaded a broad spectrum of the society involving highly educated professionals like doctors in government hospitals, school, college and university teachers, engineers, airline pilots and technicians, executives of various public sector undertakings including nationalized banks and others. These better privileged and well educated people in the organized sector periodically put pressure on their employers to accept their demands without any concern about the resultant inconvenience to the public. In the recent past, while the government had initially taken a firm stand not to yield to such threats by employees' unions, in most cases, after the strike commenced, it either succumbed to the pressure of the union, or agreed to look into some of their demands. This is a very disturbing trend.

Workers or their trade unions cannot solely be blamed for all the ills of the organized sector today. Just as there are militant trade unions, there are some unreasonable employers as well, who look for opportunities to retaliate. This scenario is not likely to change in the near future without a substantial change in the attitudes of both managers and worker's unions towards each other. Mutually acceptable terms and conditions drawn up in a strategy based on trust and respect will go a long way to ease pressure and ensure financial returns.

In 1971, the IDA was amended to add Section 11–A which widened the powers of labour courts, tribunals and the National Tribunal. Prior to this, an employer could discharge or dismiss a workman for misconduct as per the standing orders after following the procedure for conducting a domestic enquiry. The labour court/tribunal could not interfere with the quantum of punishment and act as a court of appeal in substituting its own judgement for that of the management if a fair enquiry had been conducted as per the principles of natural justice. This is now possible.

Today no employer can discharge or dismiss a delinquent workman even for serious misconduct without an elaborate procedure for taking disciplinary action. The employer can punish a workman as per the company's standing orders or the service rules only when the workman is found guilty of the charge in an enquiry conducted as per the required procedure and principles of natural justice. Even when the employer has dismissed/discharged a workman after a fair enquiry and followed the required procedure, its decision can be challenged under Section 2–A of the IDA by raising an industrial dispute. For this he need not have the support of any trade union or other workmen.

The success of any industrial organization largely depends upon the degree of discipline, efficiency and commitment of its employees. A motivated employee who willingly cooperates and observes the rules and procedures of the organization constitutes the essence of discipline in industry. This is possible only if the management is able to create a climate of trust and goodwill by its consistent policy to follow a set standard in dealing with employees uniformally, impartially and with compassion, wherever required. This almost always strengthens the managements' credibility.

ENFORCEMENT OF DISCIPLINE

It is a time-honoured tradition in every society that its members conform to a set of rules or unwritten customs based on values and ideologies. No society or organization can last unless its members behave in ways acceptable to others. There are sanctions against deviants. The objectives of discipline in industry should be to obtain acceptance of the rules and develop a spirit of accommodation and mutuality. A large number of research studies have been made on interpersonal behaviour. However, there is no conclusive answer as to why at times, a certain person behaves the way he does. Even fear of extreme penalty does not deter a criminal from committing a crime. While behavioural scientists are engaged in identifying the causes, for the present, we need to confine ourselves to the concept of discipline in industry.

It is well known that discipline cannot be enforced. Experience has shown that employees commit mistakes and as a consequence are punished. The fear of punishment however, has not been a deterrant to indiscipline. While indiscipline in industry is increasing on account of a variety of socio-political reasons, employers are convinced that under the existing legal framework, a punitive approach to maintaining discipline is no longer possible. Even after following an elaborate procedure, no employer can be certain that his decision to punish, even in a proven case of serious misconduct, will withstand judicial scrutiny. A more practical, human relations approach is probably required. This calls for education of the management personnel at various levels of the organization to understand the intricacies of human behaviour so that they can focus on achieving the organization's objectives, rather than fighting on trivial issues. Unfortunately, in the attempt to dominate subordinates, employers slip up on many basic principles in dealing with disciplinary situations, and talk only of law and procedure, even when there maybe strong mitigating circumstances to take a more lenient view. This is the principal reason why workers form a trade union to fight against the arbitrary stand of the employer.

The role played by a trade union in matters of enforcing discipline can be significant. A trade union can significantly influence the response of employees towards the management's efforts to improve productivity, reduce cost, improve quality, improve discipline among employees or for that matter change the 'work culture' in the organization. In today's context, no employer can be assured of lasting industrial harmony merely by paying higher wages, better service conditions and other benefits. Today, most employees, whether workers, supervisors or even executives (in the public sector) are part of organized trade unions which have the sanction of law.

In the past, industrial peace and production of goods and services was disrupted at many places merely because of the employer's refusal to recognize a trade union of workers even when no other economic issues were involved. Although the law in our country encourages multiplicity of trade unions and inter-union rivalry, working relations exist at many places where the management has been fair in dealing with the representative union. Further, there is no central law for recognition of a trade union. Taking advantage of the situation, many employers in the past recognized a trade union of their choice—whether it had a majority membership or not. Such a myopic view cannot ensure lasting industrial peace or labour–management cooperation. It encourages shop-floor indiscipline, multi-unionism and inter-union rivalry. There would be reasonable as well as unreasonable demands, demonstration of relative strength by various trade unions, disrupting industrial peace, causing setback to production, productivity and shop-floor discipline.

In the context of the critical employment market and due to the delay and cost involved in the judicial process, it is in the long term interests of the organization that management should deal with this vital issue more realistically than as a measure of expediency. Once the trade union is recognized, the management should enlist its cooperation in establishing various joint or bipartite forums for the settlement of employee grievances as well as those relating to production, productivity, profitability, cost reduction, safety, training for enriching employee skills and employee welfare.

These participative forums have contributed in various degrees towards maintaining industrial peace and shop-floor discipline. Since they act as channels of communication, many of the misgivings or wrong interpretation of management policies can be clarified and the cooperation of workmen and their trade unions sought. After hearing their views, the management should be prepared to amend some of its earlier decisions and approach the issues with fairness, openmindedness, objectivity and justice. This will establish its credibility in dealing with vital issues affecting workmen, and minimize problems of discipline.

The rules of discipline should be founded not on compulsion but on education and motivation. The approach should be to motivate each worker by increasing his commitment to the shared objectives through the process of empowerment. Only then would his willingness to observe rules become voluntary and discipline a part of his work culture. It is self-discipline alone which can effectively answer the challenge posed by indiscipline in our times. Once the management's credibility is established, it can even justify disciplinary action against a particularly recalcitrant person by imposing a penalty when other modes of correction have failed. Behavioural scientists have a significant role to play in this area in the coming years.

POSITIVE AND CONSTRUCTIVE DISCIPLINE

The maintenance of discipline in industry has a wide import. Every organization has a set of goals or objectives to achieve. To this end, it adopts appropriate work technology, devises policies, operating practices and procedures. Its personnel policies must be oriented towards the creation of a climate conducive to production as well as employee satisfaction. Studies by behaviourial scientists indicate that employees who work in an organization perceive the objectives, rules and policies of the organization differently. The concept of the organizational climate basically refers to the relative strength of an individual's identification and involvement with a particular organization. It has a profound influence on the employee's attitude towards the management's efforts either to improve productivity or maintain the desired level of discipline. It is a relatively enduring quality of an organization's internal environment which results from the behaviour and policies of members of the organization, especially the top management.

The internal organizational climate, which is largely influenced by the perception of employees of the managerial policies and practices determine their ultimate behaviour or outcome in terms of both performance and satisfaction. If the satisfaction level is low, indiscipline in various forms would be the likely outcome. It has also been found by behavioural scientists that a clear positive relationship exists between climate and job satisfaction. In practice, it has been found that more consultative, open, employee centered climates are generally associated with more positive job attitudes and discipline. It has been generally found that a more supportive and participative style of leadership results in increased job satisfaction, lower employee turnover, lower intra-group stress and conflict as well as higher level of discipline and increased cooperation.

For employees on the shop-floor, the front-line supervisors and plant level managers personify management. Their attitude, behaviour, style of leadership and approach in solving problems are treated by employees as a part of the managerial policy and is therefore, significant in implementing various organizational decisions including maintenance of discipline.

In any organization, although the majority of employees conform to rules and procedures and avoid misconduct, deviants exist who would have to be dealt with according to the law. Indiscipline by an individual workman is relatively simple to deal with. When it involves indiscipline by a group of employees, and/or at the instance of a trade union, its consequences may assume serious proportions and manifest in a go slow, work to rule, illegal strike, organized violence, or even sabotage or damage to plant and machinery. These may sometimes pose serious threats to industrial peace and ultimate survival of the establishment. In such a situation, it is always advisable to analyze the problem, remove the cause to the extent possible and negotiate with the trade union for a settlement on mutually acceptable terms, rather than taking recourse to disciplinary action against a large number of employees by issuing chargesheets for misconduct, or by seeking third party intervention by government machinery. Joint forums can serve the purpose of placating any outburst in the form of collective or mass indiscipline.

In an industrial set up where human beings interact as individuals as well as in groups, the object of discipline has to be preventive and corrective rather than punitive. The best rule of discipline is the Hot Stove Rule as enunciated by Douglas McGregor. According to this, a disciplinary procedure should have the qualities of a hot stove which gives out heat and glows. It is soothing in winter but warns people arounds it that if it is touched, one will get burnt. Thus, it gives an advance warning in the form of heat and at the same time punishes immediately if anyone touches it. A hot stove is impartial as well as impersonal.

Similarly, the four attributes of a good disciplinary procedure should be founded on: (*a*) advance warning; (*b*) immediacy; (*c*) impartiality; and (*d*) impersonality. An advance warning implies that employees should be aware of the rules and procedure of the organization. This calls for a proper induction system before the placement of employees in appropriate positions. The standing orders of a company provide the terms and conditions of employment, the activities which constitute misconduct and punishment for the same. Copies of the final order of the management against employees involved in serious misconduct resulting in dismissal/discharge may also be put up on the notice board which may serve as an advance warning to others.

Difficulties arise because many employees are illiterate and in many companies the standing orders are not published in the regional language. The absence of proper induction to new employees on safety and other rules and procedure applicable in many cases results in poor human relations.

The principle of immediacy calls for immediate action against indiscipline. Delay in initiating action for whatever reason may send the wrong signals and may defeat the cause of discipline. Keeping an employee suspended pending enquiry for a long time without an enquiry or final decision also demoralizes him. This tantamounts to concealed penalty although at a later date he may not be awarded the punishment of dismissal or discharge. Such delays on the part of management results in bad industrial relations. Thus, whenever any case of indiscipline occurs, the management should examine all the relevant facts, conduct a preliminary enquiry if necessary and take a decision without much delay. In some companies there is a time limit laid down to initiate and complete disciplinary proceedings.

Impartiality demands that the employer should act in good faith and with honesty in the matter of disciplinary action irrespective of the trade union affiliation or otherwise of the delinquent employee. Labour courts invariably intervene in cases where it is found that the management did not act in good faith, or it was biased in coming to its conclusion in punishing a workman, or if it was a case of victimization.

A good disciplinary procedure should be impersonal. If a fair decision is taken considering all the aspects relevant to the issue, there should be no regrets for punishing a delinquent employee for an act of misconduct proven in an enquiry conducted as per the principles of natural justice.

ROLE OF COUNSELLING

In maintaining discipline in industry, the role of counselling cannot be underestimated. Barring exceptions, human beings are not intentionally bad. We must assume that a person is good, unless otherwise proven. One solitary instance of deviation from the established rules or procedure should not be considered culpable or actionable. We must have patience as well as the desire to explore the reason for such deviation. Here, we must be objective in our approach and be prepared to listen to the employee's viewpoints, rather than make a pronouncement based on our own preconceived notions of the person or the circumstances. Our interest should be limited to establishing the gap between the standard and his actual performance. We should avoid a posture that puts the other person on the defensive. If he is wrong, in the end, he must feel so without fear of being punished. The essence is to *give the man at least one chance to improve*. We must remember that often, deviations take place because of sheer ignorance of the standard, or rules and procedures. Since the basic idea is correction, counselling could be the answer.

Good counselling almost always improves interpersonal relationships, which results in better discipline, higher productivity and greater job satisfaction. Explaining to the employees what type of behaviour would be rewarded and what would attract punishment will go a long way towards their inculcating self-discipline. The future of discipline in industry, however, would depend on the quality of leadership and the extent of commitment of the managers.

LEGAL ASPECTS OF DISCIPLINE

We are aware that even under ideal conditions, breakdowns might occur in any system. Similarly, in any industrial organization with a good record of interpersonal relations, there would be occasions when the management might have to act in conformity with law to discipline its workforce. It is, therefore, necessary to possess the required knowledge of the law and procedure to handle such contingencies effectively.

If other modes of enforcing discipline fail, we have to very clearly understand the principles, procedure and the law on disciplinary action before applying the same. No doubt this is a cumbersome and time-consuming process. Sometimes, the parties get involved in long and costly legal battles, causing harassment to both, with further appeals to higher judicial bodies.

At present, the employer-employee relationship is largely determined by the standing orders of the company certified under the Industrial Employment (Standing Orders) Act, 1946, and the Model Standing Orders, the Service Rules, or various constitutional provisions. The right to hire and fire is no longer available. These standing orders or service rules denote precisely the terms and conditions of employment and may also specify the steps that have to be taken before punishment can be decided. No employer can succeed in punishing a workman, unless he has committed an act of misconduct according to the standing orders of the company which has been proven in an enquiry.

The concept of misconduct as well as the right of the employer to take disciplinary action have also undergone substantial changes over the years. Although no legislation has been enacted so far on the subject of disciplinary action in case of misconduct, there are a large number of precedents as decided by various High Courts and the Supreme Court on principles that have to be followed before the management's action to punish an employee can be upheld as fair, reasonable and consistent with legal and constitutional provisions. Quite often, decisions of the employer, and even those of the Labour Court and High Court are reversed by the Supreme Court in appeal. At other times in a given context, the Division Bench of the Supreme Court differed with its own observations on a particular issue which had earlier settled the law. In an extreme case, both the majority view and minority view are pronounced concurrently on the same issue Union of India and Another vs Tulasiram Patel (1985 II LLJ 206 SC); Delhi Transport Corporation vs DTC Mazdoor Congress (1991 I LLJ 395 SC). All these indicate that the law on disciplinary proceedings is still in the process of evolution as per the requirements of the changing needs of society and the principles of justice and equity. Even today, the interpretation of what constitutes a fair and reasonable opportunity to defend is sometimes debated in the highest judicial forum in our country.

Based on previous case laws, the management may take disciplinary action against a delinquent workman. However, once the decision of the punishing authority is communicated to him, he can challenge it under certain circumstances by raising an industrial dispute as per Section 2–A of the Industrial Disputes Act, 1947.

Even if the management had followed the procedure laid down before inflicting punishment, it is open for judicial scrutiny before the Labour Court. These courts have been equipped with adequate powers to examine the domestic enquiry proceedings as well as the attendant circumstances relevant to the case, and decide for themselves whether the management was justified in awarding the punishment. A labour court can not only scrutinize whether the principles of natural justice have been followed and the charge established, but also act as a court of appeal with regard to the quantum of punishment. Under Section 11–A of the IDA, a Labour Court/Tribunal has the power, in appropriate cases, to reduce the quantum of punishment, even if the employer had conducted a fair and proper enquiry as per the principles of natural justice.

On this point, reference may be made to the decision of the Supreme Court in the cases of:

- Jaswant Singh vs Pepsu Roadways Transport Corporation and Another (1984 I LLJ 33 SC)
- Indian Farmers' Fertilizer Corporation Ltd. etc. vs Presiding Officer, Labour Court, Chandigarh (1999 I LLJ 1040 SC)
- U.P. State Road Transport Corpn. vs Subhas Chandra Sharma and others (2000 I LLJ 1117 SC).

In the past, in case the employer wished to challenge the award of the Labour Court reinstating a dismissed workman, it could go to the High Court in a writ under Article 226, or in appeal under Article 136 of the Constitution to the Supreme Court. Unless there was a specific directive from the higher court, the employer was not required to pay any money to the workman during the period of the proceedings. However, according to Section 17–B of the Industrial Disputes Act, 1947 (enforced from August, 1984), an employer who prefers an appeal against such award of reinstatement of a workman to a High Court or to the Supreme Court, is liable to pay full wages last drawn by the workman, pending such proceedings in higher courts.

From the foregoing it appears clear that the employers' right to take disciplinary action has been considerably curbed. No employer can be certain that his decision to dismiss a workman in a case of serious misconduct would be upheld by the Labour Court, or the higher courts, even when a domestic enquiry had been conducted as per the principles of natural justice. This is suggestive of at least one thing—that employers must be aware of the latest decisions on various aspects of disciplinary action as pronounced by the courts. Since reinstating an indisciplined workman would set a precedent cutting at the root of the management's efforts to enforce discipline, it is imperative not only that a domestic enquiry be conducted fairly as per the requirements of law, but also that appropriate punishment commensurate with the misconduct proven be awarded after following the procedure laid down, to avoid a counterproductive situation.

The following chapters deal with various facets of disciplinary action relating to the procedure to be adopted before dismissal, discharge or removal of employees based upon certain important decisions of the higher courts together with references to relevant case laws.

TWO

Misconduct and Procedure for Enquiry

EMPLOYEES' RIGHTS TODAY

In the days of laissez faire, when the master–servant relationship was predominant, the master had the absolute right to hire and fire a servant. This relationship was treated as sacrosanct and was based on predetermined terms and conditions of employment endorsed by both parties. According to this doctrine, the servant worked at the will of the master, with no subsisting right to continue in employment.

However, with the developing notions of social justice and the changed philosophy with regard to the role of the state, in order to protect the employed from exploitation various statutory restrictions were necessitated. The role of the state changed gradually from that of a silent spectator to a protector of the exploited. As the concept of the employer–

employee relationship gained ground, the employer was required to operate within the boundary of the law. Today, an employer cannot dismiss an employee without a reasonable cause, except after following a prespecified procedure.

In the case of Glaxo Laboratories (I) Ltd. vs Labour Court, Meerut and Others (1984 I LLJ 16), the Supreme Court, while discussing the provisions of the standing orders certified under the Industrial Employment (Standing Orders) Act, 1946, observed that:

> In the days of *laissez faire* when industrial relation was governed by the harsh law of hire and fire, the management was the supreme master, the relationship being referable to contract between unequals and the action of the management treated almost sacrosanct. The developing notions of social justice and the expanding horizon of socio–economic justice necessitated statutory protection to the unequal partner in the industry, namely, those who invest blood and flesh against those who bring in capital. Moving from the days when the whim of the employer was *supreme lex*, the Act took a modest step to compel by statute, the employer to prescribe minimum conditions of services subject to which employment is given. The Act was enacted, as its long title shows, to require employers in industrial establishments to define with sufficient precision the conditions of employment under them and to make the said conditions known to workmen employed by them. The movement was from status to contract, the contract being not left to be negotiated by two unequal persons but statutorily imposed.

Before terminating the services of an employee, the employer is required to conform to certain legal and/or constitutional requirements. The employer is required to satisfy the court that its action was neither arbitrary nor vindictive. Only when the employer proves to the satisfaction of the court that the delinquent employee was given a reasonable opportunity to defend himself, that there was no victimization, and action was taken in accordance to the principles of natural justice, the court may agree to uphold the management's action in a given set of circumstances.

Today, no workman can be chargesheeted and punished unless he has committed a misconduct as per the relevant standing orders applicable to him. Similarly, in the matter of disciplinary proceedings, a government servant is not only accorded constitutional safeguards under Article 311 of the Constitution, but is also statutorily governed by the Fundamental and Supplementary Rules, Civil Services Classification, Control and Appeal Rules, Government Servant Conduct Rules, etc., as applicable. He cannot be punished unless he has been given a reasonable opportunity to defend himself in an enquiry which is fairly conducted as per the norms of natural justice. The Supreme Court, while deciding the cases referred to it from time to time, has given its opinion on the definition of misconduct, the rights of employers to take disciplinary action, who should issue a chargesheet and award punishment, who should conduct the enquiry, the duties of the enquiry officer, the role of the management representatives, right of the chargesheeted employee to be represented in an enquiry and other similar issues.

WHAT IS MISCONDUCT?

Any conduct on the part of an employee inconsistent with the faithful discharge of his duties towards his employer could be misconduct. However, this must have some rational connection with his employment.

Although the expression 'misconduct' has not been defined either in the Industrial Disputes Act, 1947, or in the Industrial Employment (Standing Orders) Act, 1946, whether an act is misconduct would depend upon the certified standing orders of a company, or in its absence, on the Model Standing Orders applicable to the establishment.

Misconduct can be broadly grouped into the following heads:

1. **Misconduct relating to work:**
   - Non performance or negligence of duty
   - Absence without leave or overstaying sanctioned leave without permission
   - Absence from the appointed place of work, or being consistently tardy
   - Striking work, inciting others to strike work or provoking violence
   - Go slow, gherao, etc.

2. **Misconduct relating to discipline:**
   - Insubordination or disobedience, whether alone or along with others, or disobedience of a lawful order of the superior
   - Riotous or disorderly behaviour in relation to superiors, subordinates or colleagues
   - Other acts subversive of discipline, like rowdy conduct during duty hours, misbehaviour committed even outside duty hours but within the precincts of the establishment and directed towards the employees of the establishment, abusing superiors or co-workers or subordinates, writing anonymous letters criticising the company or the superiors
   - Drunkenness, fighting, etc.
   - Damage to employer's property or reputation

3. **Misconduct relating to loyalty and morality:**
   - Theft, fraud or dishonesty in connection with the employer's business or property, or theft of a co-employee's property or belonging
   - Misappropriation of company's property

- Disloyalty towards employer's business or reputation
- Unethical conduct and corruption
- Guilty of moral turpitude

ROLE OF THE TRADE UNION

An employee charged for misconduct may need guidance from the union in submitting a proper reply to the chargesheet. The employee may also seek the assistance of his trade union representative during the enquiry to help him in his defence in producing witnesses, other supporting evidence in his favour as well as in framing questions for cross examination of the management's witnesses. The trade union may also take up individual cases of misconduct with the management for leniency or pardon. In most places, the trade union will pursue the member employee's case at the conciliation level as well as in the labour court for reinstatement in case of discharge/dismissal. Some of the well established trade unions also grant a subsistence allowance to their members pending disposal of cases relating to discharge/dismissal before the labour court.

ENQUIRY AND THE LAW

In view of the legal implications involved and the consequences of an order of reinstatement, it is only appropriate that the decision to punish an employee should invariably be followed by an enquiry as per procedure. Since the law on the subject is still evolving, it is imperative that employers update their knowledge from time to time to avoid pitfalls which might vitiate the enquiry later. The long-term interests of the employer should be safeguarded, rather than taking a myopic view of the matter. At times there may be compelling reasons to take some urgent action against an erring employee, but knowing that the travails of law can extend to a much larger compass than what can possibly be comprehended, it is only fair keeping in mind the employer's long-term interests that expediency is given up and the rule of law followed in matters of disciplinary action. It is important that employers should be fair and reasonable before taking away an employee's means of livelihood, as it might affect his dignity and social prestige.

With the widespread unemployment scenario, the stake of an individual employee to continue working is very high. For the employer the price for reinstatement of an employee is no less. First, the organization gets back an indisciplined employee who returns as a victor without any regrets, or promises that he will amend his behavior. Second, most of the time the employer is forced to pay wages (which during these days may run into a substantial amount of money in many cases) over the period when the case is still being resolved.

Employers should therefore, address themselves clearly to these realities and act accordingly. The ruling of various High Courts and the Supreme Court reversing management decisions on disciplinary matters may be discouraging. However, this should not deter the employers. It should sharpen their vision and perspective. In this chapter, the procedure for a fair and proper enquiry is discussed.

The law now requires that an enquiry be held as per the norms of natural justice viz., *audi alteram partem* and the employee charged for misconduct must have a reasonable opportunity to:

1. deny his guilt and establish his innocence, which he can do only if he is told what charges are levelled against him; and
2. defend himself during the enquiry (with a representative in appropriate cases, if he so desires), by cross-examining the witnesses/documentary evidence produced against him and by examining himself and other witnesses, producing evidence in support of his defence.

The second principle of natural justice is the *sine qua non* for a valid enquiry and should guide the conscience of the enquiry officer. The principles of natural justice have taken deep root in the judicial conscience of our society nurtured by a number of decisions of the Supreme Court. The question whether the requirements of natural justice have been met by the procedure adopted in a given case depends on the facts and circumstances of the case in reference and the relevant rules applicable.

As held by the Supreme Court in A.K. Kripak and Others vs Union of India and Others (AIR 1970 SC 150):

> The aim of the rules of natural justice is to secure justice or to put it negatively, to prevent a miscarriage of justice. These rules can operate only in areas not covered by any law validly made.

PROCEDURE FOR ENQUIRY

The two basic principles of natural justice applicable to a domestic enquiry are (*a*) no person should be the judge in his own cause; and (*b*) to give the other side a hearing. In the absence of any law prescribing a procedure for conducting an enquiry, the principles of natural justice have supplanted the legal provisions and employers are sometimes confronted with different, and at times conflicting, judicial opinion on the same issue. Be that as it may, in the existing environment, maintainance of discipline in industry is of primary concern. Success no doubt depends on many extraneous factors. However, employers can on their part, take care to follow the correct procedure for an enquiry. Some of the basic requirements for a fair enquiry are:

1. NOTICE OF ENQUIRY

Since the objective of holding an enquiry is to give the delinquent employee a reasonable opportunity to prove his innocence as well as to defend himself, he should be given prior notice and sufficient time to prepare his defence Associated Cement Companies Ltd. vs Their Workmen, (1963, II LLJ 396 SC). For a normal case, three days may be a sufficient notice period, unless the employee requests for more time or adjournment on some specific ground, which should normally be accepted. Further, the enquiry should preferably be held during working hours and at a place easily accessible to the employee. The principle that 'justice should not only be done but should appear to have been done', should be followed to avoid imputation of the motive of prejudice/bias of the enquiry officer. The enquiry officer should issue a notice of enquiry clearly mentioning the date, time and place of the enquiry, asking the employee to be present with his witnesses/documentary evidence if any, or to give advance notice and reason for absenting himself failing which the enquiry would be held ex parte.

2. ORDER SHEET

It is necessary for the enquiry officer to keep a day-to-day record of the proceedings in the order sheet which lists the sequence in which the witnesses have been examined and cross-examined. It also includes other evidence produced and marked as such, recording dates when the enquiry was held and concluded, adjournments, if any, of subsequent sittings of the enquiry (to avoid the need for issue of a fresh notice), signatures of the concerned persons and when the findings were submitted to the punishing authority. The enquiry officer also records here that the contents of the chargesheet and its reply as well as the procedure to be followed in the enquiry have been explained to the parties concerned before starting the enquiry.

3. THE ENQUIRY

The object of holding an enquiry is to ascertain whether or not the employee is guilty of the charges levelled against him in the chargesheet. In doing so, the enquiry officer gives the employee a reasonable opportunity to defend himself by examining the witnesses/documentary evidence/exhibits produced against and in his defence. The employee can also make a statement in his defence apart from his stated reply to the chargesheet. It should be clearly understood that unless the management can prove the charge against the employee during the enquiry, he should be considered innocent. On the appointed date and time fixed for the enquiry, apart from the enquiry officer, the management representative, the chargesheeted employee (and his representative, if any) should be present with the relevant evidence in support of the case.

4. THE MANAGEMENTS' CASE

Since the burden of proof in an enquiry is on the management, it is incumbent on the management representative to produce oral as well as documentary evidence first. He should examine the management's witnesses one by one in support of the charge. They are in turn cross-examined by the chargesheeted employee. He may himself be a witness, in which case he should be the first person to depose from the management side. The management representative has a right to cross-examine the chargesheeted employee as well as the witnesses/documentary evidence produced by him.

5. THE EMPLOYEE'S CASE

If the chargesheeted employee does not accept the charge, he may produce his oral and documentary evidence to establish his innocence by submitting a reply to the chargesheet and cross-examining the witnesses/documentary evidence/exhibits produced against him and also examining his own witnesses. In certain circumstances, when the employee makes a bona fide request to the enquiry officer to arrange for some witnesses within the control of the management, the enquiry officer, after he is satisfied that such a request is reasonable, should ask the management representative to arrange for their attendance during the next sitting of the enquiry and also write to the concerned witnesses.

No enquiry can be said to have been held as per procedure in the absence of the chargesheeted employee. If, however, he refuses to take part in the enquiry after presenting himself, or does not report for the enquiry, despite receiving the notice, the proceedings may be held ex parte, provided that the notice of enquiry makes a specific mention to that effect. Further, if, during the enquiry, the chargesheeted employee withdraws his presence, the same may be held ex parte. In all such cases, however, it is advisable to postpone the enquiry and to give the chargesheeted employee another opportunity rather than holding an ex parte enquiry. In a case where the chargesheeted employee turns up for the enquiry after some witnesses have been examined, it would be proper for the enquiry officer to allow him to participate after recording this fact in the proceedings. In serious cases, the enquiry officer should recall the management witnesses who have already been examined in the absence of the chargesheeted employee so that the latter gets an opportunity to cross-examine them. It is of fundamental importance that justice should not only be done, but should manifestly be seen to be done.

Sometimes a chargesheeted employee may request for a copy of the documents mentioned in the chargesheet before submitting his explanation. As held by the Supreme Court in the case between the Committee of Management Kisan Degree College vs Shambhu Saran Pandey and Others (1995 II LLJ 625), a copy of the documents should be supplied to the delinquent employee unless they are voluminous, in which case they should be allowed to be inspected before the enquiry is held. In the event the documents cannot be supplied, the employee may obtain the appropriate extracts at his own expense. If this opportunity is not given, it would violate the principles of natural justice.

Since the entire exercise in an enquiry is directed towards giving a reasonable opportunity to the chargesheeted employee to defend himself against the allegations, it is incumbent on the enquiry officer to ensure that whatever could be considered reasonable in the circumstances of the case has been followed so that his findings are not impeached on that count at a later date. Apart from the knowledge of law and procedure, the enquiry officer has to apply his sense of justice and impartiality in deciding any issue that is raised by either party during the enquiry. He cannot take sides without importing prejudice or bias to the situation, which is not permissible. He is the best judge of dealing with a situation in a given set of circumstances. If his intentions were fair when taking a particular decision, merely because another view was possible in the same circumstances, it would not cause serious damage to the enquiry. Although courts have impeached many of the enquiries as unfair in the past, even today they give due weightage to the findings by the enquiry officer, unless it is proven that he was motivated, had acted arbitrarily, or that the findings were perverse. Since the findings of the enquiry officer may cast a stigma or lead to the dismissal of the delinquent employee, he must not act in haste to somehow complete the assignment. Patience, diligence, and a sense of justice should guide the conduct of the enquiry officer so that he may come to a balanced finding on the basis of the evidence before him. Only then would the probability of failure of such enquiries be minimized, saving the employer from consequential harassment.

RIGHT OF REPRESENTATION

The law in India does not concede an absolute right of representation as an aspect of the right to be heard, one of the elements of the principle of natural justice. In a number of cases, the Supreme Court held that there is no right to representation unless the company by its standing orders recognizes such a right. The courts favoured representation by a co-worker or a representative of the recognised union in preference to representation by a lawyer.

In the case between Kalindi (N) and Others vs Tata Engineering and Locomotive Co. Ltd., Jamshedpur (1960 II LLJ 228 SC), it was held that simple and straightforward questions of fact by a fairly intelligent person with the knowledge of conditions prevailing in the industry, as to whether acts of misconduct were committed, will ordinarily facilitate in reaching a judgement. It may often happen that the accused workman will be best suited to examine the witnesses. In the case of Brooke Bond India (P.) Ltd. vs Subbaraman (S) and Another (1961 II LLJ 417), the Supreme Court held that the workers had no right to be represented in the domestic enquiry by a counsel or by an outside agent and the refusal of the enquiry officer to permit such representation did not violate the rule of natural justice.

Similarly, in the case of Dunlop Rubber Company (India) Ltd. vs their workmen (1965 I LLJ 426), the Supreme Court held that there was no denial of natural justice because the workers had asked for representation by a member of a union which was not recognized, since the standing orders clearly provided that only a representative of a registered and recognized union could assist the workers in the enquiry.

The Supreme Court held in Cresent Dyes and Chemicals Ltd. vs Ram Naresh Tripathy (1993 I LLJ 907) that the right to be represented through a counsel or agent can be restricted by statute, rules, regulations or standing orders. A delinquent has no right to be represented through a counsel or agent unless the law specifically confers such a right. The requirement of the rule of natural justice insofar as his right of hearing is concerned does not extend to a right to be represented through a counsel or agent.

In the case of Harinarayan Srivastava vs United Commercial Bank and Another (1997 II LLJ 620 SC), it was held by the Supreme Court that a denial of opportunity to be represented by an advocate did not offend the principle of natural justice as the allegations made were simple.

Although there is no uniformity of judicial opinion on this subject as the principles involved are yet under evolution, it can be concluded that though legal representation is not an essential ingredient of natural justice in all cases, the claim for legal representation should be left to the discretion of the enquiry officer, to be allowed in exceptional cases where the facts and circumstances are complicated. If the enquiry officer is of the opinion that the refusal of legal representation would materially prejudice the defence of the chargesheeted employee at the enquiry, and is likely to result in the failure of the enquiry itself, he should permit the same.

In taking the final decision, however, the following observation of the Supreme Court in the case of the Trustees, Port of Bombay vs D.R. Nadkarni (1983 I LLJ 1) is relevant:

> In our view we have reached a stage in our onward march to fair play in action that where in an enquiry before a Domestic Tribunal the delinquent officer is pitted against a legally trained mind, if he seeks permission to appear through a legal practioner, refusal to grant this request would amount to denial of reasonable request to defend himself and the essential principles of natural justice would be violated.

FINDINGS OF THE ENQUIRY OFFICER

After the enquiry is concluded, it becomes the duty of the enquiry officer to analyze the entire evidence on record, on the basis of the chargesheet and the enquiry proceedings. He frames the issues for consideration objectively and rationally with reference to the chargesheet by looking through the evidence on record—both oral (as documented) as well as others produced in the enquiry. At the first stage, before writing the enquiry report, the enquiry officer makes exhaustive notes on various aspects including correlating specific evidence to specific issues, which part of the evidence has no relevance and the points on which there is corroborative or conflicting evidence.

At the second stage he carefully analyzes the evidence on record with reference to each issue. He may either accept or reject the evidence. In both cases he has to give his reasons for the decision. When either no evidence has been adduced on a particular point during the enquiry, or the evidence on record is conflicting, he may draw upon circumstantial evidence, if that is logical and probative. In effect, at this stage he isolates the relevant from the irrelevant evidence on each issue. He then analyzes the entire evidence with reference to all the issues (charges) for consideration and comes to a definite finding on each issue with reasons for the same. The conclusions of the enquiry officer should be logical and based upon the entire evidence before him and in particular, the charges which are substantiated. The conclusions should be based on very clear reasoning so that any unbiased person, not connected with the enquiry, would come to similar conclusions on the basis of the given evidence.

The responsibility of the enquiry officer is similar to that of a judge. He must be acquainted with the case laws on the subject relating to correct procedures so that the chargesheeted employee cannot complain of being denied of a reasonable opportunity to defend himself. As mentioned earlier, he should be fair and impartial and should not display any prejudice against the chargesheeted employee.

Since the findings of an enquiry officer can lead to the dismissal of a workman, the Supreme Court and other courts attach great importance to the conduct and findings of the enquiry officer. The courts insist that the enquiry officer must give clear reasons for the conclusions (Associated Cement Companies Ltd. vs Their Workmen (1963 II LLJ 396 SC). In the case of Anil Kumar vs Presiding Officer and Others (1986 I LLJ 101), the Supreme Court reiterated the duties of the enquiry officer to be as follows:

> A disciplinary enquiry has to be a *quasi-judicial* enquiry held according to the principles of natural justice and the enquiry officer has to act judicially. The enquiry officer did not apply his mind to the evidence. Save setting out the names of the witnesses, he did not discuss the evidence. He merely recorded his *ipse dixit* that the charges are proved. He did not assign a single reason why the evidence produced by the appellant did not appeal to him or was considered not credit-worthy. He did not permit to peep into his mind as to why the evidence produced by the management appealed to him in preference to the evidence produced by the appellant.

> Where a disciplinary enquiry affects the livelihood and is likely to cast a *stigma* and it has to be held in accordance with the principles of *natural justice*, the minimum expectation is that the report must be a reasoned one. The court then may not enter into the adequacy or sufficiency of evidence. But where the evidence is annexed to an order-sheet and no correlation is established between the two showing application of mind, we are constrained to observe that it is not an enquiry report at all. Therefore, there was no enquiry in this case worth the name and the order of termination based on such proceedings disclosing non-application of mind would be unsustainable.

Employers are often concerned that courts these days are very technical and legalistic. On matters of disciplinary action and even in serious cases involving indiscipline, they order the reinstatement of the workman for small lapses in the procedure. However equally, the requirement so fundamental to a domestic enquiry, as pointed out by the Supreme Court in the above case, should not be lost sight of by an enquiry officer.

DECISION OF THE PUNISHING AUTHORITY

After the enquiry officer submits his findings to the disciplinary authority, the latter is required to take a decision. If he agrees with the findings of the enquiry officer on the basis of the enquiry report and other connected papers, he has to decide about the next course of action. However, as held by the Supreme Court in the case of Managing Director, ECIL, Hydrabad vs B. Karunakar (1994 I LLJ 162), the principles of natural justice require that when the enquiry officer is not the disciplinary authority, the delinquent employee has a right to receive a copy of the enquiry officers' report before the disciplinary authority arrives at a conclusion with regard to his guilt or innocence. The right to make a representation to the disciplinary authority against the findings recorded by the enquiry officer is an integral part of the opportunity to defend the charges. Failure to comply would be tantamount to the denial of a reasonable opportunity to the workman to defend himself. After giving due consideration to the points raised by the chargesheeted employee if any, the disciplinary authority has to award punishment in proportion to the proven misconduct. Since his decision on this aspect of the punishment is also liable to be challenged in case an industrial dispute is raised, he should act fairly without any discrimination, or motive to victimize the workman. His decision may be guided by a study of past cases of similar nature. If the disciplinary authority takes the decision to dismiss/discharge the workman, a letter communicating the order of dismissal/discharge sets out clearly the charge(s) proven against the workman and the date from which the order is to become effective. Normally, the order of discharge/dismissal should be effective from the date of the order, unless there is an express provision in the standing orders to the contrary. The disciplinary authority, may decide to dismiss, discharge or suspend the workman for a few days, or award any other lighter punishment as per the Standing Orders, depending upon the gravity of the misconduct.

Under Section 11–A of the Industrial Disputes Act, 1947, the Labour Court has the power to reduce the quantum of punishment in appropriate cases, even when a fair and proper enquiry has been conducted. Therefore, employers should exercise adequate restraint and care before dismissing/discharging a workman. It is now well-known, that if the employer prefers an appeal to a higher court against the award of the Labour Court/Tribunal reinstating the workman, as per Section 17–B of the IDA the workman is required to be paid his full wages while the appeal is pending.

Although constitutional remedies under Articles 226 and 136 still exist for an employer to challenge the Labour Court's award in the High Court, or in the Supreme Court, once a finding of fact has been given by the Labour Court, higher courts are normally reluctant to intervene unless there are very strong grounds for the same, for example, if the conclusion is perverse, that is, based on no evidence whatsoever M. S. Dantwal vs Hindustan Motors Ltd. and Others, (1979 II LLJ 259 SC).

THREE

The Employer and his Powers

TERMINATION OF SERVICE

An employer today is not free to discipline a delinquent workman, even as per the provisions of the standing orders/service rules. He must keep in mind the principles of natural justice, the concept of reasonable opportunity for defence, the powers of a labour court, etc., under Section 11–A and Section 17–B of the IDA while dealing with his employees. In the past, employers were advised an escape route through simple termination of employees or 'discharge simpliciter'. In many instances, in order to avoid a circuitous and uncertain route, the employer took recourse to the contract of employment, the standing orders, or the service rules which allowed the employer to terminate the services of an employee by giving him notice, or paying him wages in lieu of the prescribed notice period. The labour courts required to see proof in appeal by the concerned workmen against such termination that the employers' action was bona fide and not a colourable exercise of its powers under the contract of employment. Similarly, in cases of removal from service of government employees, the High Courts and the Supreme Court examined whether or not the fundamental rights guaranteed under Article 14 and 16 of the Constitution to a government servant had been violated by the punishing authority, and whether the employer could be held guilty of arbitrary action in denying a reasonable opportunity to the employee to be heard, as required under the rules or regulations.

For many years, loss of confidence was held to be a valid ground for termination of service without following the procedure for disciplinary action. This power of the employer has now been severely restricted. Such power in the hands of the employer, either under the contract of employment, or the standing orders, or the Discipline and Service Rules has been held to be unjustified, as the employer can arbitrarily take away the employee's source of livelihood which invariably casts a stigma on him. In some cases referred to the higher courts, it was found that either the employer used this power as a pretext to get rid of an employee, even where there was no justifiable cause, or found it convenient to take recourse to such termination, as it was felt that trying to prove the guilt in an enquiry may be counter-productive. In the case of L. Michael and Another vs M/s. Johnson Pumps Ltd.(1975 I LLJ 262), the Supreme Court, while examining its earlier decisions on the subject observed that, in none of the cases the question as to the stigmatic nature of the reason for termination was either canvassed or decided. It held that:

> If termination on ground of loss of confidence could successfully pass the muster of industrial jurisprudence, it would perhaps be unnecessary for every employer to proceed against an employee for misconduct and get

involved in inordinately dilatory procedures. Every employer would be happy to merely get rid of the employee on the ground of 'loss of confidence' because in most situations an act of misconduct would, of necessity involve 'loss of confidence' or faith either in one or other of the attributes which an employee must have to be acceptable to an employer. It is, therefore, not surprising that more recent decisions have looked upon termination as ground of "loss of confidence" as being bad on the ground that it was stigmatic, and would therefore call for an enquiry even though not amounting to specifically defined misconduct under the Standing Orders, Rules, or Regulations.

The Supreme Court also held in Chandulal vs The Management of M/s Pan American World Airways (1985 II LLJ 181) that:

> It is difficult to agree with the finding of the labour court that when service is terminated on the basis of loss of confidence, the order does not amount to one with stigma and does not warrant a proceeding contemplated by law preceding termination. Want of confidence in an employee does point out to an adverse facet of his character as the true meaning of the allegation is that the employee has failed to behave up to the expected standard of conduct which has given rise to a situation involving loss of confidence. In any view of the matter, this amounts to a dereliction on the part of the workman, and therefore, the stand taken by the management that termination for loss of confidence does not amount to a stigma has to be repelled.

In some previous cases, the provisions contained in some public sector undertakings in their Conduct, Discipline and Appeal Rules relating to termination of service by giving notice, or paying salary in lieu thereof, came up for judicial scrutiny before the Supreme Court. In the case of O. P. Bhandari vs India Tourism Development Corporation Ltd. and Others (1986 II LLJ 509), the Supreme Court observed that:

> Rule 31(v) of the ITDC Conduct, Discipline and Appeal Rules, 1978 providing for termination of service by giving an employee 90 days' notice or pay in lieu thereof cannot coexist with Art. 14 and Art. 16(1) of the Constitution of India. The said rule must therefore die, so that the fundamental rights guaranteed by the aforesaid Constitutional provisions remain alive. Otherwise, the guarantee enshrined in Articles 14 and 16 of the Constitution can be set at naught simply by framing a rule authorizing termination of an employee by merely giving a notice. In order to uphold the validity of the rule in question, it will have to be held that the tenure of service of a citizen who takes up employment with the State will depend on the pleasure or whim of the competent authority unguided by any principle or policy....Such a rule is capable of robbing an employee of his dignity and making him a supine person whose destiny is at the mercy of the concerned authority (whom he must humour) notwithstanding the constitutional guarantee enshrined in Articles 14 and 16 of the Constitution of India. Therefore, Rule 31(v) of ITDC is unconstitutional and void.

A similar view was expressed by the Supreme Court in the case of Central Inland Water Transport Corporation vs Tarun Kanti Sengupta, Brojo Nath Ganguly and Others (1986 II LLJ 171). Here, Rule 9(i) of the Central Inland Water Transport Corporation Ltd. Service, Discipline and Appeal Rules, 1979, provided that the employment of a permanent employee shall be subject to termination on three months' notice in writing on either side. The company may pay the equivalent of three months' basic pay and dearness allowance, if any, in lieu of notice or may deduct a like amount when the employee has failed to give due notice. Thus, the services of a permanent employee could be terminated on the ground of 'services no longer required in the interest of the company', without assigning any reason. It was held that:

> The power conferred by Rule 9(i) is not only arbitrary but also discriminatory for it enables the Corporation to discriminate between employee and employee. They had no voice in framing the said Rules. They had no choice but to accept the said Rules as part of their contract of employment. There is gross disparity between the Corporation and its employees, whether they be workmen or officers. Rule 9(i) is a term of contract affecting a large number of persons. It is against right or reason and wholly unconscionable. It has been entered into between parties between whom there is gross inequality of bargaining power. It is harmful and unjust to public interest as it affects a large section of the public and tends to create a sense of insecurity in the minds those to whom it applies. It is opposed to public good and public policy and being opposed to public policy is *void* under Section 23 of the Indian Contract Act, 1872. It is *ultra vires* of Art. 14 of the Constitution to the extent it confers on the Corporation unreasonable and arbitrary right to terminate the employment of a permanent employee wholly ignoring and setting aside the *audi alterm partem* rule.

While commenting on the doctrine of mutuality, which confers equal rights to both sides in relation to Rule 9(i), the Supreme Court in the above case observed:

> It is true that there is mutuality in Cl. 9(i)—the same mutuality as in a contract between the lion and the lamb that both will be free to roam about in the jungle and each will be at liberty to devour the other.

In this case, the Supreme Court reviewed all the earlier decisions on the subject, confirmed those which were consistent with the decision in the present case, and overruled the rest.

To summarize, in all the government companies (there were 970 before the Supreme Court in the Central Inland W.T.C. case), wherever such an arbitrary provision existed in the service rules or regulations, enabling the company to terminate the services of an employee by giving notice or paying in lieu of notice, the same has been held to be void under Section 23 of the Indian Contract Act, 1872, as being opposed to public policy, and also ultra vires of Article 14 of the Constitution to the extent that it confers upon the company the right to terminate the employment of a permanent employee by giving him three months' notice in writing, or wages in lieu thereof. Similarly, in the case between West Bengal State Electricity Board and Others vs Desh Bandhu Ghosh and Others (1985 I LLJ 373), the Supreme Court had earlier struck down Regulation 34 of the West Bengal State Electricity Board Regulations, as violative of Article 14 of the Constitution since it conferred power on the Board to terminate the services of any permanent employee by giving three months' notice, or three months' salary in lieu of notice.

A similar provision to terminate the services of a permanent employee exists in many certified standing orders of other companies. Quite a number of cases of termination of service involving 'loss of lien' for overstay of leave, or for loss of confidence have been reviewed in the past. As stated in the PanAm's case earlier (1985 II LLJ 181), the Supreme Court is reluctant to let the employer have any sway over employment matters on the plea of contract of employment. The Supreme Court in the Central Inland Water Transport Corporation case observed that 'by entering into a contract of employment, a person does not sign a bond of slavery'.

While commenting on the role of law in a changing society, the Supreme Court in the above case observed that:

> the law exists to serve the needs of the society which is governed by it. If the law is to play its allotted role of serving the needs of the changing society, it must march in tune with the ideas and ideologies of that society. Since Constitutional amendment or the passing of law by legislative powers for changing law is a slow process, this task must, therefore, of necessity fall upon the courts because the courts can, by the process of judicial interpretation adapt the law to suit the society.

Whether it is a government company, or an instrumentality of the state as per Article 12 of the Constitution, or a company registered under the Indian Companies Act, 1956, or a society registered under the Societies Registration Act, 1860, an employer is always the stronger party as compared to the employee. Rules which were honoured in the past, and terms and conditions of employment in the standing orders certified earlier as fair and reasonable, have now to be in tune with the changing times as they are not valid or enforceable. In Workmen of Hindustan Steel Ltd and Another vs Hindustan Steel Ltd. and Others (1985, I LLJ 285), the Supreme Court examined the validity of Standing Order No. 32 of Hindustan Steel Ltd., a public sector undertaking, which provided for dispensing with an enquiry in removing or dismissing a workman. The Standing Order No. 32 read as under:

> Special procedure in certain cases: Where a workman has been convicted for a criminal offence in a Court of law or where the General Manager is satisfied, for reasons to be recorded in writing, that it is inexpedient or against the interests of security to continue to employ the workman, the workman may be removed or

dismissed without following the procedure laid down in Standing Order 31.

The Standing Order No. 31 in this case dealt with the procedure for taking disciplinary action for misconduct. The tribunal, in the dispute of termination of services of Mr. Manas Kumar Mukherjee, held that as the employer dispensed with the disciplinary enquiry in exercise of the power conferred by Standing Order No. 32, it cannot be said that the dismissal was not justified. The tribunal found the employer's action valid and accordingly rejected the reference. The party thereafter came to the Supreme Court in appeal by special leave. The Supreme Court observed that:

> This archaic standing order reminiscent of the days of hire and fire is relied upon by a public sector undertaking to sustain an utterly unsustainable order and to justify an action taken in violation of the principles of natural justice, an action which has the effect of denying livelihood and casting a stigma ... A standing order which confers such arbitrary, uncanalized and drastic power to dismiss an employee by merely stating that it is inexpedient or against the interests of the security to continue to employ the workman are violative of the basic requirements of natural justice in as much as the General Manager could impose a penalty of such a drastic nature so as to affect the livelihood and put a stigma on the character of the workman without recording the reasons why disciplinary enquiry is dispensed with and what was the misconduct alleged against the employee.

While holding that the order of the General Manager was unsustainable, the Supreme Court directed the management to recall and cancel the order of termination on the terms pronounced by it and to recast its Standing Order No. 32 within a period of two weeks, in line with the given directive to avoid further intervention. Standing Order No.

29 of the Steel Authority of India Ltd. as per which the management could dismiss an employee without holding an enquiry, came under attack for identical reasons (Steel Authority of India Ltd. and Another vs Dilip Kumar Debnath and Others 1989 I LLJ 133 SC).

Therefore, the principles of natural justice have now come to be recognized as part of the guarantee contained in Articles 14 and 16 of the Constitution also. Employers therefore no longer enjoy the right to terminate the services of an employee without following the principles of natural justice.

CIVIL SERVICE

Government servants enjoy certain protection under the Constitution against arbitrary action in matters of removal from service or reduction in rank. Provisions contained in Article 311 of the Constitution which confer certain safeguards for a government servant after the Forty-second Amendment in 1976 are as follows:

311. Dismissal, removal or reduction in rank of persons employed in civil capacities under the Union or a State:

1. No person who is a member of a civil service of the Union or an all-India Service or a civil service of a State or holds civil post under the Union or a State shall be dismissed or removed by an authority subordinate to that by which he was appointed.

2. No such person as aforesaid shall be dismissed or removed or reduced in rank except after an enquiry in which he has been informed of the charges against him and given a reasonable opportunity of being heard in respect of those charges.

   Provided that where it is proposed after such enquiry, to impose on him any such penalty, such penalty may be imposed on the basis of the evidence adduced during such enquiry and it shall not be necessary to give such person any opportunity of making representation on the penalty proposed.

Provided further that this clause shall not apply:

(a) where a person is dismissed or removed or reduced in rank on the ground of conduct which has led to his conviction on a criminal charge; or

(b) where the authority empowered to dismiss or remove a person or to reduce him in rank is satisfied that for some reasons, to be recorded in writing, it is not reasonably practicable to hold such inquiry, or

(c) where the President or the Governor, as the case may be, is satisfied that in the interest of the security of the State it is not expedient to hold such an enquiry.

(3) If in respect of any such person as aforesaid, a question arises whether it is reasonable/practicable to hold such inquiry as is referred to in Cl. (2), the decision thereon of the authority empowered to dismiss or remove such person or to reduce him in rank shall be final.

In the case of Union of India and Others vs Tulasiram Patel (1985, II LLJ 206), while examining the scope of Article 311, the Supreme Court considered all the past decisions chronologically and held as follows (para. 54):

Clause (2) of Art. 311 gives a constitutional mandate to the principle of natural justice and the *audi alteram partem* rule by providing that a person employed in a civil capacity under the Union or a State shall not be dismissed or removed from service or reduced in rank until after an inquiry in which he has been informed of the charges against him and has been given a reasonable opportunity of being heard in respect of the charges... This safeguard provided for a government servant by Cl. (2) of Art. 311 is, however, taken away when the second proviso to that Clause becomes applicable. The safeguard provided in Cl. (1) of Art. 311, however remains intact and continues to be available to the government servant. The second proviso to Art. 311 (2) was applicable in the three cases mentioned in Cl. (a) to (c) of that proviso....

Prior to the Constitutional amendment of 1976, a government employee had the right to be heard on the proposed penalty as per Clause (2) of Article 311. This provision (inserted by the Fifteenth Amendment in 1956) was deleted by the 1976 Amendment. Clause (2) of Article 311 as it was before the amendment of 1976 is reproduced below:

(2) No such person as aforesaid shall be dismissed or removed or reduced in rank except after an inquiry in which he has been informed of the charges against him and given a reasonable opportunity of being heard in respect of these charges and where it is proposed after such inquiry to impose on him any such penalty, until he has been given a reasonable opportunity of making representation on the penalty proposed, but only on the basis of the evidence adduced during such inquiry.

Thus, prior to the 1976 Amendment, a government employee had two opportunities, (a) to be informed of the charges against him and to be given a reasonable opportunity of defending himself against those charges; and (b) a reasonable opportunity of making a representation on the penalty proposed, where after such enquiry it was proposed to impose on him the penalty of dismissal, removal or reduction in rank. This second opportunity has been expressly withdrawn by the 1976 Amendment. The Supreme Court in Associated Cement Companies Ltd. vs T.C. Shrivastava and Others (1984 II LLJ 105) held that: 'Neither under the ordinary law of master and servant nor under industrial law, a second opportunity to show cause against the proposed punishment is necessary'. Since a right to such opportunity does not exist in law, it follows that a government servant can no longer claim this right.

Conclusion

With the knowledge of the safeguards an employee has in the matter of employment and job-security in India comes the importance of addressing the realities of the situation. It is naive to think that the law will in any way come to the employer's rescue, once an employee has been removed from service. Therefore, attention must be focussed on alternative ways for maintaining industrial discipline.

It is of vital importance that managers are well versed with various judicial decisions to enable them to act appropriately to protect the interests of the organization. They have to shift their stance from a traditional position of authority towards creating awareness among the workers for promoting a sense of self-discipline. The support of the recognized trade union of workmen should be solicited. In some organizations a certain period was observed for mass-contact and a no-chargesheet campaign in collaboration with the recognized trade union. During the campaign, instead of issuing a chargesheet, the concerned erring employee was called by an action group consisting of representatives of the management and the union and given counselling. A similar such system, as an ongoing process can be thought of by every organization. It is not suggested here that no chargesheet should be issued even in a case of serious misconduct, but that cases of minor and routine nature may be sent to such a joint body for counselling.

Further, there should be a joint forum at the organizational level itself to review punishment cases arising out of disciplinary enquiries. In some companies, like Tata Steel at Jamshedpur, unanimous decisions of a Zonal Works Committee, which is an appellate body consisting of equal representatives from the management and the recognized union, are binding on the management and the union. This is the principal reason why most of the employees of the company do not have to raise any industrial dispute under the Industrial Disputes Act for redressal of their genuine grievances, including punishment for misconduct.

If an in-built mechanism can be established to take care of the disputes and grievances of the employees internally, the problem of managing indiscipline will be less. Success will, however, depend much upon the top managements' support and managerial will. Till then, the problem apparently defies solution.

FOUR

Answers to 50 Frequently Asked Questions

Since the law and procedure on disciplinary action continues to change to conform to various decisions by judicial bodies including the apex court, there can be no finality about the management's action in punishing a workman. The decision of the management may be reversed if challenged, by raising an industrial dispute under the Industrial Disputes Act, or in appeal to the higher court because of lapses in the procedure, or failure to observe the principles of natural justice. Since the law on disciplinary action is still evolving, at times even when an enquiry is conducted as per the established rule or practice, some deficiencies in the procedure followed may be pointed out subsequently by the higher courts. In the circumstances, those responsible for maintaining discipline or conducting enquiries entertain doubts, solutions to which are not readily available. Some frequently asked questions have been raised with reference to the relevant case law on the subject in this chapter.

Misconduct

1. *Disciplinary action can be taken against an employee only if he is alleged to have committed an act of misconduct as per the standing orders. What does this imply?*

Misconduct has not been defined in the Industrial Employment (Standing Orders) Act, 1946, or in the Model Standing Orders. Normally, where certified standing orders exist, the acts of misconduct warranting disciplinary action spelt therein are relevant and would apply. It is difficult to lay down any general rule as to what constitutes misconduct. However, in Agnani (W.M.) vs Badridas and Others, (1963 I LLJ 684), one of earliest cases on this point, the Supreme Court had observed that in the absence of standing orders, misconduct would constitute:

- acts which are subversive of discipline amongst the employees;
- rowdy conduct in the course of working hours;
- misbehaviour committed even outside working hours but within the precincts of the concern and directed towards other employees;
- where the conduct proven against the employee is of such character that he would not be regarded as worthy of employment.

In Tata Oil Mills Co. Ltd. vs its Workmen (1964 II LLJ 113), the Supreme Court held that 'disorderly or riotous behaviour committed even outside the premises and beyond duty hours may in some cases constitute misconduct if it is connected with employment'. Further, in Mulchandani Electrical and Radio Industries Ltd. vs Workmen (1975 I LLJ 391), the Supreme Court held that under Standing Order No. 24 (1) of the company, 'assault within premises or precincts of the establishment' refers not only to the place where the act which is subversive of discipline is committed but where the consequence of such an act manifests itself.

Therefore, what constitutes misconduct, for which an employee would be liable for disciplinary action, would depend upon the relevant standing orders. Any activity not specifically enumerated in the standing orders may also be termed misconduct if it is mentioned therein that the list that is appended is only illustrative and not exhaustive, provided that the misconduct for which the employee is charged has a causal connection with his employment.

Past case laws on the concept of misconduct were reviewed by the Supreme Court in the case of Glaxo Lab. (I) Ltd. vs Labour Court, Meerut and Others (1984 I LLJ 16). In this case, the Supreme Court considered all its earlier decisions on the subject and gave a very definite direction as to the act and circumstance which would constitute misconduct in the context of the relevant provisions of the standing orders. The Court observed that as per the Industrial Employment (Standing Orders) Act, 1946, it is obligatory on the part of the employer to draw up standing orders as per the Act and in conformity with the Model Standing Orders, and define with sufficient precision those acts of omission and commission in the industrial establishment constituting misconduct, so that an employee is aware of the acts that would be construed as misconduct and carry a penalty. Against this background, the court held that:

It cannot be left to the vagaries of management to say *ex post facto* that some acts of omission or commission nowhere found to be enumerated in the relevant standing order is nonetheless a misconduct not strictly falling within the enumerated misconduct in the relevant standing order but yet a misconduct for the purpose of imposing a penalty.

Further, in the case between A. L. Kalra and Project & Equipment Corporation of India Ltd. (1984 II LLJ 186), the Supreme Court observed that the misconduct alleged against Mr. Kalra did not constitute misconduct punishable under the PEC Employees (Conduct, Discipline & Appeal) Rules, 1975, and the order for his removal from service in taking an advance for the purchase of land for house building and conveyance was set aside. In the case between Rasiklal Vaghajibhai Patel vs Ahmedabad Municipal Corporation and Another (1985 I LLJ 527), the Supreme Court took a similar view and observed:

> It is thus well-settled that unless either in the certified Standing Order or in the service regulations an act or omission is prescribed as misconduct, it is not open to the employer to fish out some conduct as misconduct and punish the workman even though the alleged misconduct would not be comprehended in any of the enumerated misconduct.

While dealing with the meaning of the term misconduct, the Supreme Court in the case between Palghat BPL & PSP Thozhilali Union and BPL India Ltd. and Another (1996 II LLJ 335) held that 'any act subversive of discipline committed outside the premises is also misconduct although an act unrelatable to the service committed outside the factory, would not amount to misconduct'.

In view of the above decisions of the Supreme Court on the concept of misconduct it would be appropriate to exercise adequate caution while initiating disciplinary action against a delinquent employee.

COMPETENT AUTHORITY

2. *It is only the competent authority who can initiate disciplinary action and award punishment. What does this mean?*

The power to take disciplinary action is specifically delegated to a competent authority. Normally, the standing orders of a company, or the service rules indicate which authority is delegated this power. In a company, there may be certain authorities who are empowered to take disciplinary action up to a particular level of employees. In many companies, the board of directors delegate the power to award punishment to employees only to the managing director or the chief executive officer, who in turn can delegate the same to other executives. The law on this point is more or less settled that it is only the *designated* disciplinary authority who is competent to take disciplinary action. If disciplinary action is taken without proper delegation, it would be invalid. In Municipal Corporation of Delhi vs Ram Pratap Singh [1976 (34) FLR], the Supreme Court held that only that person who has been delegated such authority can exercise the power to dismiss an employee.

In a case, where the punishing authority himself happens to be the complainant or witness, to avoid bias, the decision to award punishment should be taken by the authority above him.

PRINCIPLES OF NATURAL JUSTICE

3. *No enquiry can be said to have been held fairly unless the principles of natural justice have been followed in letter as well as in spirit. What does this signify?*

The principles of natural justice in a disciplinary proceeding are the cornerstone on which the entire related legal fabric is constructed. There are basically two rules of natural justice. They are:

- *nemo debet esse judex in propria causa*—no man shall be a judge in his own cause; and
- *audi alteram partem*—hear the other side.

From the above two principles emanate a number of requirements to be followed if an enquiry is to be held as fair proper and legally acceptable. The first rule stipulates that the complainant, or a person interested in the outcome of the enquiry, is not competent to conduct the enquiry. As such, a domestic enquiry should be entrusted to an impartial enquiry officer so that there is no *prejudice* or *bias* in the conduct of the enquiry and no conflict between his interest and duty. In the case between Arjun Choubey and Union of India and Others (1984 II LLJ 17), the Supreme Court examined a situation where the chargesheeted employee was dismissed by an authority who had a personal bias. The Court observed that there was a violation of the principles of natural justice, since the main thrust of the charges against the employee related to his conduct and of the disciplinary authority who passed the order for dismissal. It was not open to the latter to sit in judgement over the explanation offered by the employee. The Supreme Court held in the above case that 'No person can be a judge in his own cause and no witness can certify that his testimony is true. Anyone who has a personal stake in the enquiry, must keep himself aloof from the conduct of the enquiry'.

The second rule of natural justice is based upon the fundamental principle that no man should be condemned unheard. He should get a fair hearing, a reasonable opportunity to defend himself, which includes the chance to prove his innocence Tripathy K. L. vs State Bank of India and Another (1984 I LLJ 2 SC). This includes a reasonable opportunity envisaged by the provision to:

- deny his guilt and establish his innocence, which he can only do if he is told what the charges levelled against him are and the allegation on which such charges are based;
- defend himself by cross-examining the witnesses produced against him and by examining himself or any other witnesses in support of his defence; and finally

- make his representation as to why the proposed punishment should not be inflicted on him which he can only do if the competent authority furnishes a copy of the findings of the enquiry officer to the delinquent after the enquiry is over.

Therefore, in a domestic enquiry held as per the required procedure, where the workman has been found guilty of a serious act of misconduct and the punishing authority agrees with the findings of the enquiry officer, before he arrives at a conclusion with regard to the guilt of the employee and communicates the punishment, he is required to furnish a copy of the enquiry officer's report to the delinquent employee *even when it has not been asked for, or when the statutory rules do not permit furnishing of such report, or are silent* Managing Director, ECIL Hyderabad vs B. Karunakar (1994 I LLJ 162 SC). This provision, incidentally, is applicable to all establishments—whether government, non-government, public or private sector.

4. *How are the rules of natural justice sought to be followed in a domestic enquiry?*

There is a lot of confusion on this issue even today. Based on the two basic principles of natural justice as narrated above, it follows that a domestic enquiry should aim at gathering facts relating to the chargesheet and drawing a conclusion strictly on the basis of the evidence adduced during the enquiry. The mode of collecting the facts is also equally important.

Since an enquiry is required to be conducted fairly and properly, caution should be exercised from the beginning. An individual who has to perform this quasi-judicial function as an enquiry officer, should not have any interest in the outcome of the domestic enquiry. He can also be an outsider (Indian Telephone Industries Ltd. vs Devi Shankar Kumar Shukla (2000 I LLJ 531 SC). He should be guided by justice and fair play and be open-minded, without prejudice or bias against the chargesheeted employee, who should be given a reasonable opportunity to defend himself in the enquiry. What constitutes 'reasonable opportunity' in a given situation, however, would depend on the facts and circumstances of the case. For example, in the matter of proper representation the same standard could not be applicable for an illiterate person which could otherwise be considered just and fair in the case of an educated person facing an enquiry. In the case of J. K. Agarwal vs Haryana Seeds Development Corporation Ltd. (1991 II LLJ 412), the Supreme Court held that the right of representation by a lawyer may not in all cases be a part of natural justice. Also, in the case of Harinarayan Srivastava vs UCO Bank and Another (1997 II LLJ 620), the Supreme Court observed that there would be no violation of the principles of natural justice if no lawyer is permitted to represent as the charges were very simple. However, the Supreme Court also observed that denial of representation of the workman by a lawyer in certain circumstances could vitiate the enquiry Board of Trustees, Port of Bombay case (1983 I LLJ 1 SC).

In Sur Enamel and Stamping Works vs The Workmen (1963 II LLJ 367), the Supreme Court held that an enquiry has not been properly conducted unless:

1. the employee has been clearly informed of the charges levelled against him;
2. the witnesses are examined—ordinarily in the presence of the employee);
3. the employee is given a fair opportunity to cross-examine the witnesses;
4. the employee is given a fair opportunity to examine witnesses including himself, in his defence, if desired; and
5. the enquiry officer records his findings citing the reasons in his report.

PRELIMINARY ENQUIRY

5. *Sometimes a preliminary enquiry is conducted before a chargesheet is issued. What is the status of such enquiry in relation to a disciplinary enquiry after the issue of the chargesheet?*

   The object of a preliminary enquiry is to ascertain whether there are grounds, *prima facie*, for initiating disciplinary action, and if so, to frame appropriate charges. Such an enquiry cannot be compared with a regular enquiry which is usually held after the explanation of the chargesheet is received. The necessity to conduct a preliminary enquiry depends on the nature of the alleged misconduct and in private industries, it is not necessary to hold one in all cases.

6. *A detailed preliminary enquiry was held in a theft case and the statements of all the concerned persons were recorded in the presence of the workman involved who was given an opportunity to cross-examine the witnesses. The workman accepted his mistake and a chargesheet was issued. Is it necessary to hold a domestic enquiry in this case, or can the management award him punishment straight away?*

   The object of a preliminary enquiry is limited to ascertaining whether there are grounds *prima facie*, for issuing a chargesheet, and to frame appropriate charges. Although a detailed preliminary enquiry was held here, it cannot substitute the proceedings in a regular enquiry. In the certified standing orders of a company as well as in the Model Standing Orders, there is a provision for conducting an enquiry after the receipt of reply to the chargesheet. The principles of natural justice also require that such a course be followed. The statements recorded during the preliminary enquiry have no evidential value unless they are produced in the course of the regular enquiry as per the procedure laid down by the Supreme Court in Kesoram Cotton Mills vs Gangadhar (1963 II LLJ 371).

In Depot Manager, Andhra Pradesh State Road Transport Corporation, Medak, vs Mohd. Ismail and Another (1997 I LLJ 1192), the Andhra Pradesh High Court held that a preliminary enquiry is of a very informal character and the methods are likely to vary in accordance with the requirements of each case. The delinquent employees have no vested right in any form or procedure of holding a preliminary enquiry. The procedure is wholly at the discretion of the officer holding the enquiry, who need not record his satisfaction in writing nor give reasons for initiating the regular departmental enquiry. A preliminary enquiry does not result either in exoneration or punishment and should not affect any of the legal rights of the delinquent employee.

COUNTER COMPLAINT IN ASSAULT CASES

7. *In the event a workman involved in the assault of a supervisor or a co-worker during working hours registers a counter-complaint, how are such cases to be handled?*

When a workman is issued a chargesheet for assaulting his supervisor, sometimes he files a counter complaint against the complainant, as part of his defence. In such a case, it is always advisable to conduct a preliminary enquiry for recording statements of the eye witnesses. If it is found that a *prima facie* case exists against both, they should be chargesheeted. Otherwise, only the guilty should be chargesheeted.

SUSPENSION PENDING ENQUIRY

8. *Sometimes, an employee is suspended to facilitate the enquiry of a chargesheet and is paid a subsistence allowance during the period of suspension. Can it be*

inferred from this action that the management punished the employee because it was biased?

Suspension pending enquiry is not a punishment as held by the Supreme Court in Laxmi Devi Sugar Mills vs Ram Swaroop and Others (1957 I LLJ 17). It involves only a temporary suspension of the contract of employment and is not an implied right. There has to be some specific provision either in the contract of employment, or the standing orders, or any other statutory rule applicable to the establishment regarding scale of payment during suspension (Balwantrai Ratilal vs State of Maharashtra (1968 II LLJ 700 SC). If such an express provision is not there, the employer is required to pay full wages to the employee for the period of suspension (W. S. Dhamankar vs Cantonment Board, Belgaum (1985 II LLJ 485 Karnataka). Reference may also be made to the case of T. Kajee vs U. Jormanik Siem (1961 I LLJ 652 SC).

Normally, in industrial establishments where the provisions of the Industrial Employment (Standing Orders) Act, 1946, are applicable, there should be a clause on this subject in the certified standing orders. However, after the amendment of this Act in 1982, a new Section 10–A has been added, providing for payment of a subsistence allowance to all employees covered by the standing orders of the establishment during the period of suspension pending enquiry, whether such a provision exists in the certified standing orders or not. To discourage employers from delaying enquiries, the rate of the subsistence allowance, which is 50 per cent of the wages for the first 90 days, is automatically enhanced to 75 per cent of such wages, if the enquiry proceedings get prolonged beyond 90 days in case the delay is not directly attributable to the conduct of such employee. There may be industrial establishments to which the provisions of the Act relating to certification of standing orders may not be applicable. For them, unless this power is created by a statute governing the contract or an express term in the contract itself, the employees will have to be paid full wages for the entire period of such suspension Hotel Imperial New Delhi vs Hotel Workers' Union (1959 II LLJ 544 SC).

ROLE OF ENQUIRY OFFICER AND MANAGEMENT REPRESENTATIVE

9. *What is the role of the enquiry officer and the management representative in an enquiry?*

In the past, when the law on disciplinary enquiry was not too clear, the management appointed an enquiry officer to conduct the enquiry in respect of the charges, as per procedure. The enquiry officer ascertained whether the chargesheeted employee was guilty or not by giving an opportunity to both sides to produce evidence and allowing cross-examination by the opposite party. He was free to seek clarification from the concerned witness and the party affected by such a clarification had the right to cross-examine the witness. At that time, the enquiry procedure was rather simple and the formalities to be observed were few. Since the enquiry officer had to play the role of a judge, he was required to be free from any prejudice or bias. An enquiry was considered to be a domestic affair of the employer except that certain procedures and norms of natural justice had to be followed Associated Cement Companies vs Their Workmen and Another (1963 II LLJ 396 SC).

However, with the passage of time, decisions of various High Courts and the Supreme Court on various aspects of the domestic enquiry were pronounced. From a domestic affair, it became a quasi-judicial matter, although the higher courts held the view that the rules of evidence as contemplated in the Evidence Act,

1872, were not applicable to a domestic enquiry in the same manner as they apply in a criminal trial Union of India vs T. R. Varma (1958 II LLJ 259 SC). The substantive rules of evidence that are at the root of the principles of natural justice however, have to be followed Central Bank of India Ltd. vs Prakash Chandra Jain (1969 II LLJ 377 SC). For example, in a domestic enquiry also, the burden of proof is on the management. Hence, the order of examination of witnesses and their cross-examination as per the procedure in the Evidence Act, cannot be ignored in a domestic enquiry. However, as held by the Supreme Court in the case of the Employers of Firestone Tyre and Rubber Co. (I) Ltd. vs their workmen (1967 II LLJ 715), in a domestic enquiry, the delinquent can be asked before any evidence is led against him only in a clear case, that is, when the accusation is based on a matter of record or the facts are admitted in reply to the chargesheet. In such a case, it is permissible to draw the attention of the chargesheeted workman to the evidence on record against him which, if he cannot satisfactorily explain, must lead to a conclusion of guilt. In certain cases, it may even be fair to the delinquent to take his version first, so that the enquiry may cover the points of difference and the witnesses may be questioned properly on the aspect of the case suggested by him. It is all a question of justice and fair play. It is, however, wise to ask the delinquent whether he would like to make a statement first or wait till the evidence of management witnesses is over.

As mentioned earlier, the role of the enquiry officer in a domestic enquiry is that of an impartial judge. Since his findings may take away the livelihood of an individual, it is his duty to act impartially and give a reasonable opportunity to the chargesheeted employee to defend himself, not only by being able to controvert the managements' evidence but also produce his own to prove his innocence. Since justice and fair play in action are the two basic requirements, the enquiry officer should guard against any act by which prejudice might be caused to the defence of the chargesheeted employee. Also, he should not appear to have been gathering evidence or facts in support of the management's case Andhra Scientific Co. Ltd. vs Seshagiri Rao and Another (1961 II LLJ 117 SC). Justice should not only be done but *appear* to have been done. The enquiry officer can be an official of the company, or a lawyer engaged by the company Saren Motors (Pvt.) Ltd. New Delhi vs Viswanath and Another (1964 II LLJ 139 SC), or even an outsider, as held by the Supreme Court in Indian Telephone Industries Ltd. vs Devi Shanker Kumar Shukla (2000 I LLJ 531), but care should be taken to appoint only such a person as enquiry officer who is neither a witness nor is personally interested in any way in the matter for which the chargesheet has been issued. The general principle that he must not only be a party to the proceedings but must have no legal or pecuniary interest in them however small, or such a favour as would create a real likelihood of bias, should be borne in mind.

Since, the burden of proof is on the management, it is incumbent on it to adduce sufficient evidence in the enquiry in support of the charge. As such, the management is required to nominate a person as a management representative or presenting officer in the domestic enquiry. The management representative can be the complainant himself, or any other responsible person who is conversant with the facts of the case. He is the custodian of the management's case, like the public prosecutor in a criminal trial. He does everything required to prove that the chargesheeted employee is guilty by producing relevant evidence both oral as well as documentary, in support of the charge. Apart from examining the managements' witnesses and producing documentary evidence and exhibits in support of the charge, he also cross-examines the evidence and witnesses produced by the chargesheeted employee. In fact, the management representative plays a distinct role in the enquiry to justify the management's case. In view of various judicial pronouncements, this role can no longer be played by the enquiry officer without showing prejudice.

10. *After a preliminary enquiry, two employees alleging assault against each other during duty hours were chargesheeted. What will be the role of the management representative in the enquiry?*

Strictly speaking, there is very little the management representative can do in such a case. He will explain the circumstances leading to the issue of the chargesheets and produce the relevant complaints of the employees and the statements recorded during the preliminary enquiry. The respective chargesheeted employee will examine his own witnesses and cross-examine the witnesses of the other party. In this case, both chargesheeted employees will be present throughout the enquiry.

DRAFTING AND ISSUE OF CHARGESHEET

11. *What are the requirements of a proper chargesheet? If a workman does not reply to the chargesheet within the prescribed time limit, will it be proper to issue another chargesheet to him?*

A chargesheet must contain the exact nature of the allegation and/or the material facts. If it relates to an incident, the date, time and place, and the names of the persons involved should be mentioned. In case it relates to facts based on documentary evidence, details of the same, and in appropriate cases, photocopies should be attached with the chargesheet. The relevant clause of the standing order/service rule according to which the act of the employee is a misconduct, should also be indicated.

The chargesheet should be precise, lucid and comprehensive. The employee's guilt of the misconduct admitted to in the preliminary enquiry does not need to be mentioned as it would reflect that the punishing authority has already prejudged the case, and in issuing a chargesheet he is only completing a formality. A time limit for a written reply should be indicated. (See the case study in Annexure 3).

The chargesheet duly signed by the disciplinary authority should be served on the workman personally if possible, and acknowledgement to that effect obtained. In case the workman is absent, or refuses to accept the chargesheet it should be sent to his local and home addresses by registered post with acknowledgement due, after getting his refusal attested by two witnesses. In case the chargesheet is returned unserved with the remarks of the postal authorities, the same should be kept intact without opening and the employer should display the chargesheet on the notice board or act in accordance with the provisions of the standing orders. In some cases, it may be necessary to publish the contents of the chargesheet in a local newspaper having wide coverage. After a chargesheet has been served on a workman, he may submit his explanation within the time specified for the reply:

- admitting the charges and requesting for mercy;
- denying the charges and requesting for an enquiry;
- not submitting any explanation at all; or
- requesting for more time to submit an explanation.

In case the workman admits the charge, which is of a minor nature, and requests for mercy, and there is no doubt that the reply is voluntarily written without persuasion or pressure no enquiry need be held. A decision can be taken, either pardoning him, or letting him off with a minor punishment and warning not to repeat such misconduct. If however, the misconduct is serious enough to warrant discharge or dismissal, the management should still arrange to hold a proper enquiry, not withstanding the admission of the charge.

In a case where the workman submits an explanation mentioning that the charges levelled against him are false, baseless, or motivated, an enquiry should be held as per procedure before awarding any punishment.

When the workman fails to submit any explanation within the specified time limit, the management should take steps to hold a proper enquiry after ensuring that the chargesheet has been received by him.

When the workman makes a bona fide request for extension of time to submit an explanation, it should be granted.

On expiry of the period within which the employee was to submit his explanation, the management may issue him a notice of enquiry, drawing attention to the chargesheet and his failure to reply; further informing him of another opportunity to defend himself, and that an enquiry officer (whose name should be indicated) has been appointed to conduct the enquiry on a particular date, time and place. A copy of the chargesheet along with the notice of enquiry should be enclosed. The notice of enquiry should mention that if the employee does not attend the enquiry on the appointed date and time with his witnesses and documentary evidence if any, the enquiry will be held ex parte. Although in some companies, the standing orders may provide for issuing a fresh chargesheet for not replying to the first chargesheet, instead the employee may be advised in the notice of enquiry itself to give his explanation if any, before commencement of the enquiry.

12. *Is it necessary that in respect of a civil servant the charges should be framed by the authority competent to award the proposed penalty?*

The issue whether the initiation of the disciplinary proceedings and the final decision to award punishment in respect of a public servant is to be done only by the appointing authority has been examined by the Supreme Court in the following cases:

- State of Madhya Pradesh vs Shardul Singh (1970) 1 SCC 108: [1971 Lab I.C. (N) 5].
- P. V. Srinivasa Sastry vs Comptoller and Auditor General (1993) 1 SCC 419: (1993 AIR SCW 550).
- Transport Commissioner, Madras vs A. Radha Krishana Moorthy (1995) 1 SSC 332: (1995 AIR SCW 1555).
- Inspector General of Police and Another vs Thavasiappan (AIR 1996 Supreme Court 1318).

Under Article 311(1) of the Constitution, a civil servant shall not be dismissed or removed by an authority subordinate to that by which he was appointed. Penalty in all such cases should be imposed only by an authority competent to exercise this power. However, an authority other than the one competent to impose the proposed penalty can initiate the departmental proceeding as well as conduct the enquiry.

REQUIREMENTS FOR A FAIR PROCEDURE FOR ENQUIRY

13. What constitutes a fair procedure in a domestic enquiry?

The following steps should be followed for a fair and proper enquiry:

1. The enquiry officer should read out the chargesheet and the employee's explanation. If he has accepted the charges in his written explanation, he should be asked if he has understood the charges and confirms the reply as true and final. If he has denied the allegations in his written explanation, the enquiry

officer should ask the employee if he will accept the charges or not. In case he accepts the charges, his statement may be recorded first and the management representative allowed to cross-examine him. If the charges are of a serious nature, the management representative should produce his witnesses and documentary evidence/exhibits if any, on which the management's allegations are based. The chargesheeted employee should be given an opportunity to cross-examine in each case. Necessary endorsement on the order-sheet should be made by the enquiry officer relating to the sequence of events during the enquiry and signatures of the concerned persons taken.

2. In case the chargesheeted employee denies the charge before the enquiry officer, the only course is to proceed with the enquiry even in a case where in reply to the chargesheet the employee had accepted the charges. In that event, after making necessary endorsements on the order-sheet, the enquiry officer should explain the procedure to be followed in the enquiry and call upon the management representative to produce his witnesses one by one for examination and cross-examination apart from submitting the exhibits/documentary evidence if any, in support of the charge. These should be suitably marked as exhibits and the chargesheeted employee should be afforded an opportunity for inspection and cross-examination.

The chargesheeted employee should be similarly asked by the enquiry officer to produce documentary evidence/exhibits if any, and also his witnesses. After each witness has been examined the management representative should be allowed to cross-examine. Finally, the chargesheeted employee should be asked if he wishes to give a statement which should be recorded and the management representative should be given opportunity to cross-examine the chargesheeted employee. Once the chargesheeted employee/the management representative completes the cross-examination, the enquiry officer should make an appropriate endorsement on the proceedings. This will preempt the possibility of the proceedings being challenged on the plea that the chargesheeted employee/management representative was not given an adequate opportunity for cross-examination.

3. Since the object of a domestic enquiry is to find out the facts and not to prove the charge levelled against the workman (as some people believe), the enquiry officer should record the statement of the management witnesses before the charge-sheeted workman is asked to make any statement in his defence, or disclose the names of his witnesses (in advance) to be examined during the enquiry. The underlying principle behind such a course is, that the management representative or the complainant has to prove the charge against the workman concerned by adducing sufficient evidence, and not for the chargesheeted workman to prove that he is not guilty. If however, the chargesheeted workman is closely cross-examined before any evidence has been led against him, it would appear that the intention of the enquiry officer was not fair. Normally evidence should be recorded in the presence of the concerned workman which serves very useful purpose. First the witness is cautious in giving evidence against the chargesheeted workman in his presence. Second, there is no room for persuading the witness to give a false statement. It is also always easier for the chargesheeted workman to cross-examine any witness if the evidence is recorded in his presence Kesoram Cotton Mills vs Gangadhar and Others (1963 II LLJ 371 SC).

4. Although the enquiry officer normally confines himself to ensuring that the proceedings are held as per the requirements of law, at times it becomes necessary for him to seek clarification of the witness to clear bona fide doubts to help him reach a correct conclusion. The enquiry officer should be cautious and guard against any temptation of seeking clarification the reply to which might go towards justifying the charge against the employee. If such a situation is apparent on record, it might be concluded later by the labour court that the enquiry officer was biased and took upon himself the responsibility of the management representative in bringing home the charge. The chargesheeted employee has a right to cross-examine such a witness after the enquiry officer has sought clarification.

5. In a domestic enquiry, it is the responsibility of the parties concerned and not of the enquiry officer to ensure that witnesses are made available. In fact, the officer holding a domestic enquiry could take no effective steps to compel the attention of a witness. Tata Oil Mills Co. Ltd. vs its Workmen (1964 II LLJ 113 SC). If however, some witnesses cited by the chargesheeted employee are relevant to the case and within the control of the management, the enquiry officer should request the management representative to have them released for the enquiry and also write to the witnesses about the request of the chargesheeted employee.

6. If the employee requests for representation by a co-worker, an official of the trade union or lawyer, depending upon the nature of the charges and rules applicable to such enquiry, the enquiry officer should permit such representation as the circumstances may require. Although the law on this point is still not settled, it should be remembered that acceding to the request for representation of a

lawyer may not be necessary in all cases. However, in appropriate cases where a chargesheeted employee is pitted against a legally trained mind (like a CBI Inspector), or when the presenting officer of the management or the management representative is a lawyer or when the charges involve complicated questions of law or fact, a refusal of the employee's request to engage a lawyer would amount to a denial of reasonable opportunity and vitiate the enquiry. In all other cases where the company's standing orders/service rules are silent on this point, if the employee wants to be assisted by a co-worker during the enquiry, the request should be accepted.

7. As the enquiry progresses, the enquiry officer should obtain on each page of the proceedings the signatures of the chargesheeted employee and his representative, if any, the concerned witness and of the management representative. Prior to this the enquiry officer, should explain the statements to the chargesheeted employee and the concerned witness in a language understood by them and make an endorsement to that effect with his signature.

8. As already stated, the object of the domestic enquiry is to conform to the *audi alteram partem* principle of natural justice. If all the steps that have been followed are consistent with this requirement, the enquiry is fair, otherwise it can be impeached as unfair and all efforts of the enquiry officer would be in vain. Any disciplinary action taken on such an enquiry is destined to fail.

14. *Sometimes an employee may request for the proceedings of the enquiry to be recorded in the vernacular as stated during the enquiry, rather than translated and recorded in English. Is it necessary to accede to such a request? What is the legal position on this?*

By and large, workers are illiterate or semi literate, and may request the enquiry proceedings to be recorded in the regional language or in Hindi so that they may conduct their defence properly. In the Model Standing Orders Schedule–1 under the Industrial Employment (SO) Central Rules, 1946, as well as under the Maharashtra Recognition of Trade Unions and Prevention of Unfair Labour Practices Act, 1971, the proceedings of an enquiry are to be recorded in Hindi, Marathi, English or the language of the state, whichever is preferred by the workman. There should be no hesitation in recording the proceedings in the language understood by the workman. In other cases, the law as such does not recognize the right of a workman for the chargesheet to be served, or proceedings recorded in a language known to him. In the case of Woodbriar and Sussex Estates vs Their Workmen (1960 II LLJ 673), the Madras High Court held that there is no obligation to take down evidence either in a regional language or in the language known to the employee, unless there is statutory provision in this regard. In the absence of any statutory provisions relating to the procedure in a domestic enquiry, the only obligation of a person conducting the enquiry is that he will have to act according to the rules of natural justice, giving the employee an opportunity for adequately representing his case.

15. *Can the enquiry officer decline examination of a witness cited by the delinquent employee?*

There may be an occasion when the chargesheeted employee may want to produce a certain witness in defence. In the normal course, in order to give a reasonable opportunity to the chargesheeted employee to defend himself there should be no objection to examining such a defence witness who might help mitigate the charge. There may be occasions when the enquiry officer may disallow producing such a witness when he bona fide comes to the conclusion that the said witness would be irrelevant to the enquiry. However, if the refusal appears to be the result of the desire on the part of the enquiry officer to deprive the person charged of an opportunity to establish his innocence, that would be a very serious matter Ananda Bazar Patrika (P) Ltd. vs Their Employees (1963 II LLJ 429 SC).

ENQUIRY OFFICER AS WITNESS

16. *Can a person, who has been a witness to the incident for which an employee has been chargesheeted, be competent to conduct a domestic enquiry?*

Since the duty of the enquiry officer is to act as an impartial judge in conducting the domestic enquiry, he should be neither a witness nor a person interested in the outcome of the case. A person who has witnessed an incident, may appear in the domestic enquiry as a witness and not as an enquiry officer.

The domestic enquiry must be conducted honestly and bona fide with a view to determining whether the charge against a particular employee is proven or not and care must be taken to see that these enquiries do not become empty formalities. If an officer claims that he had himself seen the misconduct alleged against an employee, in fairness, steps should be taken to see that the task of holding an enquiry is assigned to some other officer who is not likely to impart his personal knowledge to the proceedings which he is holding as enquiry officer Associated Cement Companies Ltd. vs Their Workmen and Another (1963 II LLJ 396 SC).

17. *Can the enquiry officer disallow any question by a chargesheeted workman in the cross-examination?*

The relevance of a question at the domestic enquiry is to be decided by the enquiry officer. In case the enquiry officer feels that the chargesheeted employee is asking irrelevant questions or those which have already been answered merely to prolong the enquiry, he may disallow the same. Unless it is shown that he was acting mala fide in disallowing some questions which were relevant, it would not vitiate the enquiry. As long as the enquiry officer has given reasonable opportunity to the chargesheeted employee to defend himself, the enquiry procedure cannot be held to be unfair.

LEADING QUESTIONS

18. *Can a leading question be asked in a domestic enquiry?*

A leading question suggests the answer in the question itself and such questions are not permitted when the management representative examines management witnesses or when the chargesheeted employee examines his witnesses. The only exception is that while deposing, the concerned witness speaks against the party producing him. For example, if any management witness gives evidence in favour of the chargesheeted workman, the management representative can draw the attention of the enquiry officer and declare him to be a hostile witness. Thereafter, such a witness produced by the management can be cross-examined by the management representative. It is a similar case with a chargesheeted employee.

In a domestic enquiry, the enquiry officer should ensure that during the examination-in-chief of witnesses, questions are not asked which may give a clue to the answer. Such leading questions should not be allowed to be answered at this stage but there is no bar in asking leading questions during cross-examination.

SUMMONING OF WITNESSES BY ENQUIRY OFFICER

19. At times, a delinquent employee may request the enquiry officer to call senior executives of the company as defence witnesses. Should the enquiry officer agree?

As has been stated before, the enquiry officer cannot deny the chargesheeted employee a reasonable opportunity to defend himself. What is a reasonable opportunity would depend on the circumstances of each case. Although as per the earlier law on the subject, since the enquiry officer had no power like a civil court to summon any witness, it was incumbent on the parties to produce their own witnesses, during the enquiry Tata Engg. & Locomotive Co. Ltd. vs S. C. Prasad (1969 (19) FLR 150 SC); Tata Oil Mills Co. Ltd. vs Their Workmen (1964 II LLJ 113 SC).

Lately, there has been a shift in the thinking on the subject. It is still not considered the duty of the enquiry officer to ensure the attendance of any person whose name has been given to him by the chargesheeted employee, as observed by the Andhra Pradesh High Court in Nellimerla Jute Mills Co. Ltd. vs Labour Court, Guntur (1981 (59) FJR 315). The principles of natural justice would however, be violated if the workman requests the enquiry officer to examine a particular witness and this request is denied, even though it may be possible to comply with. Therefore, in the event a chargesheeted employee makes a bona fide request to the enquiry officer for calling some employees or executives of the company as his witnesses, the enquiry officer if satisfied that it is expedient to do so, must write to the persons so named and the management representative mentioning the request of the chargesheeted employee. A copy of the above communication should be given to the chargesheeted employee after recording the same in the order sheet. Thereafter, it is for the chargesheeted employee to arrange for the production of such witnesses in the enquiry.

REPRESENTATION OF WORKMAN BY LAWYER

20. *In the event a chargesheeted employee requests the assistance of a lawyer in a domestic enquiry, is the enquiry officer bound to allow such representation?*

Since the management is usually well represented, there should be no objection towards permitting a chargesheeted employee to be represented in the enquiry as he may not be conversant with the intricacies of the procedure followed. In some companies, the rules provide representation of the chargesheeted employee by a union committee member of the recognized trade union, or in his absence, by a co-worker. The point of representation of a delinquent employee in a domestic enquiry by another employee of the same establishment was examined by the Supreme Court in Bharat Petroleum Corporation Limited vs Maharashtra General Kamgar Union and Others (1999 I LLJ 352). It was held that a co-employee of the same establishment in which the delinquent is employed, would be fully aware of the conditions prevailing in the parent establishment, its service rules, including the standing orders and would be in a better position than an outsider to assist the delinquent in the domestic proceedings for a fair and early disposal.

Lately however, there has been a demand for representation by an independent lawyer. A few cases on this point have been decided by the High Courts and the Supreme Court where it has been observed that since the chargesheeted workman is pitted against a legally trained mind or a qualified lawyer playing the role of the management representative/presenting officer, the denial of a similar privilege to the chargesheeted employee will tantamount to denial of reasonable opportunity to defend himself and ultimately vitiate the enquiry itself and violate the principles of natural justice. In Board of Trustees, Port of Bombay vs Dilip Kumar Ragvendranath Nadkami and Others (1983 I LLJ 1), the Supreme Court took the same view.

In the case of M/s. India Photographic Co. Ltd. vs Saumitra Mohan Kumar (1984 I LLJ 471), the Calcutta High Court observed as follows:

> Though the court should discourage involvement of legal practitioners in simple domestic enquiries, like disciplinary enquiries, for avoiding complication and delays, yet the court cannot ignore the necessity of such a representation in exceptional cases where refusal of such representation would constitute failure of the enquiry itself. Principles of natural justice demand conceding such a claim. No general rule can be laid down in this respect but the issue must be left for consideration the light of the facts and circumstances of each individual case.

'In Venkataraman Sambamurty vs Union of India and Another (1986 II LLJ 62), the Bombay High Court examined the issue of legal assistance to the delinquent in a domestic enquiry. In this case, the prosecuting officer was a high ranking CBI officer and the chargesheeted employee asked for permission to engage a lawyer. This request was rejected. It was held that though the prosecuting officer was not a legal practitioner as commonly understood, he was an experienced officer with a number of domestic enquiries to his credit where he had acted as a prosecutor. Because of his experience, the prosecuting officer had a legally trained mind. The Court held that there was a violation of the principles of natural justice because the balance in favour of the prosecutor would indeed be considerable, to the extent of tilting the enquiry against the chargesheeted employee. A similar view was taken by the Madras High Court in Pushpa Iyangar vs Indian Airlines and Others (1988 I LLJ 385). In the case of Union of India vs Karunakaran Nair (1986 I LLJ 124), the Kerala High Court observed as follows:

Normally, a lawyer has no place in a disciplinary enquiry. But when the presenting officer, even if he is not a lawyer, is one who is well-trained in the prosecution work, and if the delinquent officer cannot have the services of a legally trained person and is allowed to have only the services of a colleague, who in the normal course will not be well-versed in the subject, it goes without saying that, that will be nothing but denial of an opportunity to the delinquent to defend himself in the enquiry. The presenting officer need not be a lawyer for the delinquent officer to insist that he should be allowed to make use of the services of a lawyer. The presenting officer need only be a person trained in the technique of a disciplinary enquiry.

The Supreme Court in J. K. Agarwal vs Haryana Seeds Development Corporation Ltd. (1981 II LLJ 412), held that the right of representation by a lawyer may not in all cases be a part of natural justice and no general principle valid in all cases can be enunciated.

In K. N. Shukla vs Bharat Heavy Electricals Ltd. (1989, I LLJ 374), the Delhi High Court held that:

The mere fact that the presenting officer was holding a law degree does not mean that he was a practising lawyer so as to entitle the delinquent officer to have the assistance of a legal practitioner. The charges against the officer were not complicated and they involved only questions of fact. Therefore, there is nothing wrong in the management's declining the request of the employee for engaging the services of a lawyer. In fact, the delinquent officer in this case had cross-examined the witnesses and therefore, it cannot be said that any prejudice has been caused to the officer concerned by not permitting him to have the assistance of a lawyer.

The entire case law on the subject of representation of a workman in a departmental proceeding was reviewed

by the Supreme Court in Bharat Petroleum Corporation Ltd. vs Maharashtra General Kamgar Union and
Others (1999 I LLJ 352). It was held that a delinquent
employee has no right to be represented by an advocate in departmental proceedings, and that if the right
to be represented by a co-workman is given to him,
the departmental proceedings would not be vitiated
only for the reason that the assistance of an advocate
was not provided to him. Further, in Cipla Ltd. and
Others vs Ripu Daman Bhanot and Another (1999 I
LLJ 900), the Supreme Court confirmed that a delinquent employee had no right to be represented by an
advocate in the departmental proceedings.

ON CROSS-EXAMINATION

21. *What is the object of cross-examination in a disciplinary enquiry? Is the enquiry officer bound to allow cross-
examination by a chargesheeted employee or is there
some limit?*

The principles of natural justice require that the
chargesheeted employee should be afforded a reasonable opportunity to defend himself by cross-examining
the management's evidence—both oral, as well as
documentary. His efforts in the course of cross-examination are directed towards rebuttal and testing the
veracity of the management's witness, thereby trying
to convince the enquiry officer that the testimony of
the witness is not reliable. He may also try to establish enmity between the witness and himself to suggest that credence could not be given to his evidence.
He may also try to contradict the versions of different
management witnesses with the same object. Denial of
such an opportunity would amount to denial of a reasonable opportunity. Ananda Bazar Patrika (Pvt.) Ltd.
vs Their Employees (1963 II LLJ 429 SC).

Sometimes, the chargesheeted employee might ask irrelevant or personal questions in a cross-examination solely to humiliate a witness. This should not be permitted. However, before rejecting such a question, the enquiry officer should ask him about the relevance of such a question. The employee may sometimes try to prove some relevant fact about the credibility or character of the witness to dilute the evidentiary value of his testimony. In dealing with such situations, the enquiry officer should act impartially and with an open mind. If he really feels that the question was totally out of context and disallowing such a question would not cause any prejudice to the chargesheeted employee's defence, he may decide to do so. He may use a similar discretion, when the chargesheeted employee asks repetitive questions. It is all a matter of justice and fair play and the enquiry officer is the best judge to decide such issues in the given circumstances. However, if at a later date, it is found that in disallowing certain questions in cross-examination, the enquiry officer was actuated by a desire to deny a reasonable opportunity to the employee to defend himself, or that it has caused prejudice to his defence, that would mean denial of a reasonable opportunity to defend Municipal Corporation of Greater Bombay vs R.D. Tulpule and Others (1979 54 FJR 372 Bombay HC).

OBJECT OF THE ENQUIRY

22. What is the basic objective of holding a domestic enquiry?

The basic objective of a domestic enquiry is to gather facts relevant to the chargesheet in order to ascertain whether the chargesheeted employee is guilty of the allegation or not. No employer can succeed in dismissing an employee (even when he has committed a serious act of misconduct) without an enquiry as per procedure, by appointing an enquiry officer in consonance with the principles of natural justice. Even then, as held in Indian Iron & Steel Co. Ltd. vs Their Workmen (1958, I LLJ 260 SC), the Labour Court/Tribunal has the power to intervene when:

(a) there is a want of good faith;

(b) there is victimization or unfair labour practice;

(c) the management has been guilty of a basic error or violation of a principle of natural justice; and

(d) the finding is completely baseless or perverse.

The cardinal principle behind such an enquiry is that *no man should be condemned unheard*. In other words, when the management produces its evidence in support of the charge, the chargesheeted employee should be given a reasonable opportunity to defend himself which may even mean representation by a lawyer in certain circumstances. It may also be necessary for the enquiry officer to call certain witnesses, within the control of the management whose evidence in the enquiry may support the chargesheeted employee's contention, if the latter makes such a request. In a situation where the enquiry officer examined a witness on his own to clarify doubts on any issue, he must give the chargesheeted employee an opportunity to cross-examine such a witness. Otherwise, there would be a violation of the principles of natural justice Graphite India Ltd. vs State of West Bengal and Others (1980 II LLJ 29 Calcutta). Since the chargesheeted employee is to be considered not guilty, unless the mangement has been able to justify the allegation by adequate evidence, the duty of the enquiry officer is to record the evidence in an impartial way without causing any prejudice to the chargesheeted employee's case. It should be clearly understood that the object of a domestic enquiry is not to prove the charge, but to ascertain the facts relevant to the case to come to a correct conclusion which is most probative in the circumstances.

CHANGING THE ENQUIRY OFFICER

23. *Can a chargesheeted employee object to the appointment of an enquiry officer who found the employee guilty in an earlier enquiry that resulted in punishment of the concerned employee?*

Merely because an officer had conducted an enquiry in the past against the same employee in which he was found guilty and punished, would not warrant changing the enquiry officer. However, if such an allegation is made, the courts might go for a closer scrutiny of the conduct of the enquiry officer, to ascertain whether he exhibited any prejudice and whether the principles of natural justice were observed in giving a fair opportunity to the employee to defend himself during the enquiry.

A chargesheeted employee may object to the appointment of a particular person as enquiry officer, imputing motives to him or suggesting a closed mind, implying that the employee did not expect impartial treatment. After considering the reasons given by the chargesheeted employee and other attending circumstances, the employer has to take a conscious decision, whether or not there is some real apprehension of any bias to the employee, if the enquiry officer was not changed. In case the disciplinary authority holds the view that no prejudice is likely to be caused, he need not change the enquiry officer and can inform the employee of his decision.

AUTHENTICITY OF THE RECORD OF ENQUIRY

24. *Can a workman take a plea after fully participating in the enquiry that the proceedings were not correctly recorded by the enquiry officer?*

This point was examined by the Supreme Court in the case of Digwadih Colliery vs Ramji Singh (1964 II LLJ 143). To avoid such an allegation, the enquiry officer should ask the chargesheeted workman to sign on all the pages after explaining the same to him during the enquiry in a language he understands. In case the workman refuses to sign even after the contents are explained to him, the enquiry officer should make an endorsement to this effect in the proceedings and get the same attested, if witnesses are available.

As held by the Supreme Court in the above case, if a domestic enquiry is conducted fairly, the conclusions reached, on the basis of the factual position cannot be questioned unless it is characterized as perverse. The mere fact that the concerned workman has challenged the accuracy of the record of the proceedings of the enquiry, would not imply that the record was inaccurate. Therefore, when the enquiry officer recorded that the concerned workman had declined to cross-examine a witness, the tribunal could not conclude that the enquiry was unfair simply because the workman alleged that he was not allowed to cross-examine the witness.

SUBMISSION OF LIST OF EVIDENCE/WITNESSES

25. *Is it proper for the enquiry officer to ask both the management representative and the chargesheeted employee to submit their list of evidence/witnesses at the commencement of the enquiry?*

No. It is neither desirable nor necessary to adopt such a course of action. Both sides should have the freedom to decide what evidence/witnesses to produce, without disclosing the same in advance either to the enquiry officer, or to the other party. In the event the list of witnesses and/or evidence is known in advance, the chargesheeted workman may, after seeking an adjournment of the enquiry, try to persuade or pressurize the witnesses and influence their testimony. Similarly, it might be alleged that the management may have tried to influence the testimony of the charge-sheeted workman's witnesses. This will vitiate the atmosphere of the enquiry, apart from inviting criticism that the enquiry officer was unjust.

Since the concept of reasonable opportunity involves not only giving a fair chance to the employee to defend himself by cross-examining the management's witnesses and by producing his own witnesses, he should not be asked to give the names of his witnesses beforehand, unless he makes a request to the enquiry officer to call such witnesses, who are vital for his defence, and within the control of the management. In all other cases, after the cross-examination of the management's witnesses the enquiry officer should ask the chargesheeted employee to produce his witnesses one by one.

DOMESTIC ENQUIRY AND CRIMINAL TRIAL

26. *Sometimes, after the notice of enquiry has been issued, the chargesheeted employee may request for keeping the enquiry in abeyance on the plea that he is facing a criminal trial on the same issue. In the past, depending on the nature of the misconduct, the enquiry proceedings could either be held or stayed. What is the current position on the subject?*

There is no material change in the legal position on the subject of holding a parallel domestic enquiry when a criminal case on the same issue is pending trial before a criminal court. In Delhi Cloth & General Mills Ltd. vs Kushal Bhan (1960 I LLJ 520), the Supreme Court clearly stated that, 'the principles of natural justice do not require that an employer must at least wait for the decision of the criminal trial court before taking action against an employee'.

Having stated thus, the Supreme Court also observed that in a case of a grave nature, it is advisable for the employer to await the decision of the trial court so that the defence of the employee in the criminal case may not be prejudiced. In Tata Oil Mills Co. Ltd. vs Their Workmen (1964 II LLJ 113), the Supreme Court reiterated this stand. Also, in Jang Bahadur Singh vs Baijnath Tewari (1969 I LLJ 567), the Supreme Court confirming its earlier two decisions (DCM and TOMCO referred to above) held that:

> The power of taking such action is vested in the Disciplinary Authority. The civil or criminal court has no such power. The initiation and conclusion of disciplinary proceedings in good faith is not calculated to obstruct or interfere with the course of justice in the pending court proceedings. The employee is free to move the court for an order restraining the continuance of the disciplinary proceedings. If he obtains a stay order, a wilful violation of the order would of course amount to contempt of court. In the absence of a stay order, the Disciplinary Authority is free to exercise its lawful powers.

In Kusheswar Dubey vs M/s. Bharat Coking Coal Ltd. and Others (1988 II LLJ 470), the Supreme Court reiterated its earlier three decisions referred to above. It held that:

> The view expressed in the three cases of this court seems to support the position that while there could be no legal bar for simultaneous proceedings being taken, yet, there may be cases where it would be appropriate to defer disciplinary proceedings awaiting disposal of the criminal case. In the latter classes of cases, it would be open to the delinquent

employee to seek such an order of *stay* or *injunction* from the court. Whether in the facts and circumstances of a particular case there should or should not be such simultaneity of the proceedings would then receive judicial consideration and the court will decide in the given circumstances of a particular case as to whether the disciplinary proceedings should be interdicted, pending criminal trial. As we have already stated, it is neither possible nor advisable to evolve a hard and fast straight-jacket formula valid for all cases and of general application without regard to the particularities of the individual situation.

Regarding the holding of a disciplinary enquiry after the acquittal on a charge by the criminal court, the full bench of the Karnataka High Court in T.V. Gauda vs State of Mysore (1975 II LLJ 513), held that there is no bar for holding disciplinary enquiry even after acquittal on a charge by the criminal court. This view was confirmed by the Supreme Court in the case of Corporation of Nagpur vs R.G. Modak (AIR 1984 SC 626).

In this connection, reference may also be made to the cases of P. J. Sundararajan and Another vs Unit Trust of India and Another (1993 I LLJ 65 SC); Depot Manager, APSRTC vs Md. Yusuf Mia etc. (1997 II LLJ 902 SC) and State of Rajasthan vs B. K. Meena and Others (1997 I LLJ 746 SC), in which the Supreme Court, reiterating its earlier view, held that it is not desirable to lay down inflexible rules regarding which departmental proceedings may be stayed and which may not. There would be no bar to proceed simultaneously with the departmental enquiry of a criminal case unless the charge in the criminal case is of a grave nature involving complicated questions of fact and law.

In Capt. M. Paul Anthony vs Bharat Gold Mines Ltd. and Another (1999 I LLJ 1094), the Supreme Court reviewed its prior decisions as well as those of various

High Courts and held that while the employer is not required to stay the disciplinary proceedings pending a criminal trial against the employee, if the case is of a grave nature or involves complicated questions of fact and law, it would be advisable for the employer to await the decision of the trial court, so that the 'defence of the employee in the criminal case may not be prejudiced'. In other cases, the parallel proceedings can go on, as proceedings in a criminal court and the departmental proceedings operate in distinctly separate jurisdictional areas. In the departmental proceedings, where a charge relating to misconduct is being investigated, the standard of proof required in such proceedings is different than that required in a criminal case. While in departmental proceedings the standard of proof is one of preponderance of the probabilities, in a criminal case, the charge has to be proven by the prosecution beyond a reasonable doubt. In Sr. Superintendent of Post Offices Palthanamthitta and Others vs A. Gopalan (1999 I LLJ 1313), the Supreme Court confirmed this position. As such, even if a person gets acquitted in a criminal trial, it would not automatically entitle him for reinstatement if he has been dismissed for a serious act of misconduct.

JOINT ENQUIRY

27. *In one case, several workmen were issued separate but identical chargesheets for causing a disturbance and assaulting security guards during duty hours. Is it necessary to hold separate enquiries for each chargesheet?*

Although there is no fixed rule, the management may sometimes find it expedient to hold separate enquiries, although the chargesheeted employees may demand a common enquiry.

APPLICABILITY OF THE EVIDENCE ACT

28. *The rules of evidence as per the Evidence Act, 1872, are not applicable in a disciplinary enquiry, as maintenance of internal discipline and administration is still considered to be within the domain of the employer. We are also aware of the fundamental rights and constitutional guarantees of employees, the necessity of providing a reasonable opportunity to defend, arbitrary and unreasonable powers of the employer, etc. The procedure for a disciplinary enquiry has been held to be a quasi-judicial function by the highest court in this country. We have neither the talents available nor the time required to get involved in such long drawn and cumbersome proceedings. For efficient functioning, as well as the continued existence of any industrial organization, there must be discipline at all levels. The arduous path of enforcing discipline through chargesheet, enquiry etc., is well known. To tackle the problem:*

- *appoint legally trained persons in the organization and entrust disciplinary enquiries to them;*

- *suspend an employee charged with serious misconduct pending enquiry and after his reply is received dismiss him without enquiry. After all, as per Section 11–A of the Industrial Disputes Act, the management can justify its action before the labour court/ tribunal by adducing fresh evidence. By this action can the employer save itself of current as well as future harassment?*

As early as 1958 when the law on domestic enquiry began to take definite shape, in Union of India vs T.R. Varma (1958 II LLJ 259), the Supreme Court observed that a domestic enquiry is to be held as per the principles of natural justice and not as per the procedure laid down in the Indian Evidence Act, 1872, as followed in a court of law. This point was elucidated in the case of Central Bank of India Ltd. vs Prakash Chandra Jain (1969 II LLJ 377), when the Supreme Court held that although the technical rules of evidence as contained in the Evidence Act were not applicable to a domestic enquiry, the substantive rules of evidence that emanate from the principles of natural justice could not be ignored. Recording evidence at an enquiry in the presence of a chargesheeted person to substantiate a fact is a requirement of the substantive rule of evidence based on the *audi alteram partem* principle of natural justice. Similarly, the concept of burden of proof which is dealt with under Sections 101–103 of the Evidence Act, are also applicable in a domestic enquiry, inasmuch as if the management failed to prove the charge against the employee by adducing evidence during the enquiry, he is to be held not guilty, even if he has not adduced any evidence to prove his innocence. The order of examination of witnesses in support of the charge as contained in Sections 135 and 138 of the Evidence Act, is also to be followed in a domestic enquiry.

As stated earlier, employees, whether in government services, public corporations, or industrial establishments in the private sector, have now substantial legal protection against arbitrary or unjust treatment at the hands of their employers. The courts have and will continue to intervene, with the so-called right of the employer under the contract of employment to terminate the services of an employee. This is a reality and perspective that we can no longer be oblivious of. The provisions of the Industrial Disputes Act, 1947, as amended from time to time, is a reference in point. In the past, awards of the labour courts/tribunals in hundreds of cases of dismissal of workmen went in favour of the workmen but may have been reversed in appeals before higher courts. However, now, as per Section 17–B of the Industrial Disputes Act, if the employer prefers an appeal to a higher court against the order of reinstatement of the workman by the labour court/ tribunal, he is required to pay full wages last drawn to the workman during the pendency of the appeal. This reflects the collective thinking of our parliament which passed this law.

Some companies employ lawyers to conduct enquiries and represent them in the labour courts, etc. However, dispensing with the domestic enquiry altogether is fraught with serious consequences. Proceedings before a labour court are similar to other proceedings in a court of law. The standing orders or service rules of a company provide the procedure for taking disciplinary action for misconduct. No employer should violate the provisions of the certified standing orders, which have the force of law. As held by the Supreme Court in Workmen of M/s Firestone Tyre and Rubber Co. Ltd. vs The Management and Others (1973 I LLJ 278), under Section 11–A, the employer can lead fresh evidence to justify its action in dismissing a workman, in that:

> The expression 'materials on record' occurring in the proviso to Sec. 11–A cannot be confined only to the matters which were available at the domestic enquiry...

> They take in,

> (i) the evidence taken by the management at the enquiry and the proceedings of the enquiry, or
>
> (ii) the above evidence and, in addition any further evidence led before the Tribunal, or
>
> (iii) evidence placed before the Tribunal for the first time in support of the action taken by an employer as well as the evidence by the workman contra.

The Supreme Court also held in the above judgement that:

> We should not be understood as laying down that
> there is no obligation whatsoever on the part of
> an employer to hold an enquiry before passing an
> order of discharge or dismissal. This Court has
> consistently been holding that an employer is to
> hold a proper enquiry according to the standing
> orders and principles of natural justice... Further,
> by holding a proper enquiry, the employer will
> also escape the charge of having acted arbitrarily
> or malafide... Further, it will also enable the em-
> ployer to persuade the tribunal to accept the en-
> quiry as proper and the finding also as correct.

So, which course of action would cause less harassment
to the employer? The two options include conducting
a fair enquiry at the company level, or dismissing a
workman without enquiry. The latter option is per-
haps shortsighted in that, after a few years he would,
in all probability, be reinstated with back wages by
the labour court/tribunal. Other consequences an employer would face when dismissal is effected without
enquiry are disruption of industrial peace, allegation
of victimization, etc.

Why aren't Enquiries Carried out by Lawyers?

29. *With the procedure and the law on disciplinary proceedings becoming more complicated, will eventually enquiries be carried out by lawyers?*

It would be unfortunate if disciplinary enquiries are
entrusted solely to legally trained persons. In this
event, the employee would also have to be given the
right to be represented by a lawyer. The observations
of the Supreme Court in Board of Trustees, Port of
Bombay's case (1983 I LLJ 1 SC) are relevant. In paragraph eight of the judgement, it is observed that:

The time-honoured and traditional approach is that a domestic enquiry is a managerial function and that it is best left to the management without the intervention of persons belonging to legal profession. This approach was grounded on the view that a Domestic Tribunal holding an enquiry without being unduly influenced by strict rules of evidence and the procedural juggernaut should hear the delinquent employee in person and in such an informal enquiry, the delinquent officer should be able to defend himself. The essential assumption underlying this belief is questionable but it held the field for some time and there are decisions of this Court in Brooke Bond India (Pvt.) Ltd. vs Subba Raman (S) and Another (1961, II LLJ 426), in which it has been held that in a disciplinary enquiry before a Domestic Tribunal a person accused of misconduct has to conduct his own case and, therefore, as a corollary it cannot be said that in such an enquiry against a workman, natural justice demands that he ought to be represented by a representative of his union much less a member of the legal profession. While buttressing this approach, an observation was made that unless rules prescribed for holding the enquiry do not make an enabling provision that the workman charged with misconduct is entitled to be represented by a legal practitioner, the Enquiry Officer and/or the employer would be perfectly justified in rejecting such a request as it would vitiate the informal atmosphere of a Domestic Tribunal.

In paragraph nine of the judgement, the Supreme Court observed as follows:

Even in domestic enquiry there can be very serious charges and adverse verdict may completely destroy the future of the delinquent employee. The adverse verdict may so stigmatize him that his future would be bleak and his reputation and livelihood would be at stake. Such an enquiry is generally treated as a managerial function and the Enquiry Officer is more often a man of the establishment. Ordinarily he combines the role of a Presenting cum Prosecuting Officer and an Enquiry Officer, a judge and a prosecutor rolled into one. In the past, it could be said that there was an informal atmosphere before such a Domestic Tribunal and that strict rules of evidence and pitfalls of procedural law did not hamstring the enquiry by such a Domestic Tribunal. We have moved far away from this stage. The situation is where the employer has on his payrolls labour officers, legal advisers, lawyers in the garb of employees and they are appointed Presenting-cum Prosecuting Officer and the delinquent employee pitted against such legally trained personnel has to defend himself. Now, if the rules prescribed for such an enquiry did not place an embargo on the right of the delinquent employee to be represented by a legal practitioner, the matter would be in the discretion of the Enquiry Officer whether looking to the nature of charges, the type of evidence and complex or simple issues that may arise in the course of the enquiry, the delinquent employee in order to be able to afford a reasonable opportunity to defend himself, should be permitted to appear through a legal practitioner.

Domestic enquiry is claimed to be managerial function. A man of the establishment dons the robe of a Judge. It is held in the establishment's office or a part of it. Can it even be compared with the adjudication by an impartial arbitrator or a court presided over by an unbiased Judge? Witnesses are generally the employees of the employer who directs an enquiry of the misconduct. This is sufficient to raise serious apprehensions. Add to this uneven scales, the weight of legally trained minds on behalf of the employer simultaneously denying that opportunity to delinquent employee. The weighted scales and tilted balance can only be partly restored if the delinquent is given the same legal assistance as the employer enjoys. Justice must not only be done but seem to be done is not an euphemism for the courts alone, it applies with equal vigour and rigour to all those who must be responsible for fair play in action and a quasi-judicial Tribunal cannot view the matter with eqanimity or inequality of representation.

The above decision of the Supreme Court has set the tone of the requirements relating not only to the representation of workmen in a disciplinary enquiry but also the enquiry itself. The employer may choose the lesser evil among the two alternatives.

Why Conduct an Enquiry?

30. *As per Section 11–A of the IDA the employer can continue to justify its action against a delinquent workman by adducing fresh evidence. Why don't employers adopt this course rather than getting entangled in a long-drawn out legal procedure that causes nothing but harassment in the process?*

It appears that courts in India are still of the view that employees, whether in the public or private sector are the weaker section and are exploited by their employers. With so many constitutional guarantees available to a government employee, the existing laws and the concept of reasonable opportunity which is still in the process of evolution, there is an urgent need to review the entire law on disciplinary proceedings in order to maintain discipline in industries. Given the employers' right to hire and fire, on the one hand, and the employees' right for protection against unfair treatment on the other, the level of discipline is the only casualty. The relevance of holding a disciplinary enquiry only to have every aspect of it microscopicly analyzed later is questionable. Till the late sixties, the domestic enquiry was a simple affair. It has now become a highly specialized and a quasi-judicial formal proceeding. For government employees, the employer in appropriate cases can take recourse to termination without enquiry as given in the proviso to Article 311(2) of the Constitution.

Section 11–A, of the Industrial Disputes Act, 1947 is not meant for doing away with the domestic enquiry before dismissal of a workman. The chances of any employer succeeding before the labour court in its action of dismissal without holding an enquiry is remote and allegations of mala fides, victimization and unfair labour practice will be made. It will also be against the provisions of the standing orders applicable to the workmen, cannot be justified as legal or proper and is therefore, not recommended.

There are some who nurture the thought that irrespective of pleadings, when a disciplinary enquiry is held to be invalid, the tribunal is under an obligation to give an opportunity to the management to substantiate the charge by adducing fresh evidence. This is not true. As observed by the Supreme Court in Cooper Engineering Ltd. vs P. P. Mundhe (1975, II LLJ 579) and Shankar Chakraborty vs Britannia Biscuit Co. Ltd. (1979 3 SCC 371), the tribunal has no such obligation and its decision on this point would be subject to specific pleading at the appropriate stage of the proceeding before the labour court/tribunal Delhi Cloth and General Mills Co. Ltd. vs Ludh Budh Singh (1972 I LLJ 180 SC).

31. *Is the complex procedure for disciplinary action worthwhile taking in every case?*

It must be kept in mind that the right of the employer to discharge or dismiss a workman is subject to various statutory restrictions. In many cases in the past, action taken by the employer has been set aside, either because the proper procedure for the enquiry was not followed, the principles of natural justice were violated, or the punishment was disproportionate to the misconduct proved. The law on industrial disputes has been amended from time to time, putting more restrictions on the employers' right to take disciplinary action and giving more powers to the labour court/ tribunal to intervene in disciplinary matters. Therefore, in industrial establishments, where the employers' right to dismiss a workman is clearly restricted the procedure for conducting an enquiry cannot be bypassed before punishing an employee with discharge or dismissal.

Outsider as Witness

32. *Can a non-employee be examined as a witness in a domestic enquiry?*

If he is a material witness and is willing to be examined, he can be produced by either party to give testimony. The enquiry officer however, cannot compel his attendance, if he refuses to appear as a witness in the domestic enquiry.

Ex Parte Enquiry

33. *Often, an ignorant or misguided chargesheeted employee does not cooperate with the enquiry officer. He may ask for repeated adjournments on some pretext or the other; not respond to the notice of enquiry at all; or, at the instance of the trade union representative, walk out of the enquiry*

*without putting his signature on the proceedings for
the day (although recorded in his presence). What is the
procedure for handling such contingencies?*

This kind of behaviour is not unusual. By and large,
employees are ignorant of the procedural aspects of a
disciplinary enquiry, and are usually guided and
represented by their trade union in an enquiry.
According to the principle of *audi alteram partem*, if the
chargesheeted employee is not present, there cannot
be a valid enquiry. To preempt such a possibility, the
notice of enquiry itself should indicate that if the
employee does not attend the enquiry on the appointed
date and time without showing sufficient cause in
advance, the same would be held ex parte. Requests
for adjournments on bona fide grounds, like ill health
or the temporary unavailability of important witnesses,
should normally be granted keeping the circumstances
in mind. The enquiry officer should take a fair decision.
On an occasion where the enquiry officer genuinely
feels that the employee is trying to avoid the enquiry,
he may proceed ex parte after informing the employee
Tata Oil Mills Co. Ltd. vs Their Workmen (1964 II LLJ
113 SC).

In the event an employee leaves an enquiry during the course of the proceedings without signing the
statements recorded before him, instead of holding
the enquiry ex parte it would be proper to adjourn the
enquiry. In the notice of enquiry, the enquiry officer
should clearly record this and give him one more
chance on the date and time indicated. If the employee
did not attend the enquiry on that date, it could then
proceed ex parte. In Mohd. Shahid vs Aligarh Muslim
University and Another (1998 I LLJ 25), the Supreme
Court held that withdrawal from enquiry by the
delinquent employee does not give the freedom or
absolve the enquiry officer from holding ex parte enquiry according to law. A mere absence of the employee
or his refusal to participate may not be regarded as

proof of the charges. Once the ex parte enquiry is over, the enquiry officer is required to submit his findings to the disciplinary authority, who in turn should forward a copy of the enquiry report to the chargesheeted employee for his views, if any, before administering punishment.

34. *Can an ex parte enquiry be conducted in a case where the delinquent employee refuses to accept a chargesheet notice of enquiry, or is not available for personal service and the chargesheet notice of enquiry which is sent to his local and/or home address by registered post with acknowledgement due returns undelivered.*

If an employee refuses to accept a chargesheet or notice of enquiry, the procedure laid down in the company's standing orders or service rules should be followed. In some cases, the rules provide sending the same by registered post with acknowledgement due to the employees' local and/or home address available with the company. In other cases, the rules provide posting a copy on the notice board, or sending the copy to the recognized trade union. However in the absence of specific guidelines, the company should publish the contents of the notice in a local newspaper with wide publicity, as held by the Supreme Court in Bata Shoe Co. (P) Ltd. vs D. N. Ganguly (1961, I LLJ 303). Subsequently, if the employee does not reply to the chargesheet or attend the enquiry, it could then be held ex parte.

It is however, prudent to avoid holding an ex parte enquiry unless there is no other alternative, as in such an enquiry the principle of *audi alteram partem* is said to be on the 'shelf'. If the enquiry is carried out in a hurry and the employee is not present to defend himself, the court might hold that the entire enquiry proceeding was unfair and bad in law. The concerned employee should be given two or three chances to appear at the enquiry. Before holding an ex parte enquiry, it should also be ensured that the employee received the notice of enquiry on time, with the clause that it would be held ex parte if he did not attend without showing sufficient reasons in advance.

In Union of India and Others vs Dinanath Shantaram Karekar and Others (1998 II LLJ 748), the Supreme Court reviewed a case where the chargesheet which was sent to the delinquent employee was returned with the postal endorsement 'not found'. It was held to indicate that the chargesheet was not tendered to the respondent even by the postal authority. A document sent by registered post can be treated to have been served only when it is established that it was handed over to the addressee. Where the addressee was not available even to the postal authorities, and the registered cover was returned to the sender with the endorsement 'not found', it cannot be legally said to have been served. The management should have made further efforts to serve the chargesheet on the chargesheeted employee. Initiating the departmental proceedings only after a single effort was inappropriate. The show cause notice was sought to be served to the delinquent employee by publication in a newspaper without making a concerted effort to serve it to him personally by the office peon or by registered post. There is nothing on record to indicate that the newspaper in which the show cause notice was published was a popular newspaper or that it had a wide circulation in the locality where the employee lived. The Supreme Court held that the show cause notice cannot, therefore, in these circumstances be held to have been served on the employee.

Further, in State of Uttar Pradesh and Another vs T. P. Lal Srivastava (1997 I LLJ 831), the Supreme Court held that even where no reply is submitted by a chargesheeted employee, the disciplinary authority is not absolved of the duty to hold an ex parte enquiry to find out whether or not the charge is proven. In case the enquiry officer finds that the charge is proven, the disciplinary authority should communicate a copy of the enquiry report to the delinquent employee and seek his views on the proposed action. If the chargesheeted employee submits any explanation, the same should be taken into consideration before passing an appropriate order. A similar view was taken by the Supreme Court in the case between UP (Madhya) Ganna Beej Evam Vikas Nigam Ltd. and Others vs Prem Chandra Gupta and Others (2000 1 LLJ 1052), where on the basis of an ex parte report by the enquiry officer, the concerned employee was dismissed without furnishing him with a copy of the enquiry report, thereby denying him the opportunity to make a representation against the report.

HOSTILE WITNESS

35. *Often during an enquiry, a witness being examined on behalf of the management, changes side and gives a statement in support of the chargesheeted workman. There are also instances where, either the complainant or an eye-witness does not disclose relevant facts in support of a charge, due to persuasion or threat from the other side. How are these situations dealt with?*

In order to avoid such an unpleasant situation, the management representative should thoroughly brief all management witnesses prior to the enquiry. In case a witness is afraid or threatened, his protection should be arranged to the extent possible. If after these precautions, the witness speaks in favour of the chargesheeted employee, he should be declared a 'hostile witness' by the management representative, who should then be permitted to cross-examine him to obliterate the evidentiary value of his testimony. The chargesheeted employee also has the right to cross-examine the hostile witness. A similar procedure should be followed if a witness produced by the chargesheeted employee becomes hostile during the enquiry.

SECTION 17–B

36. *According to Section 17–B of the Industrial Disputes Act, 1947, a workman who has been reinstated by the labour court/tribunal is required to be paid his last drawn wages pending appeal by the management in higher courts. There have been different interpretations on what constitutes 'last drawn wages'. What is the correct position?*

There have been conflicting decisions of judicial bodies on what constitutes 'full wages last drawn'. In Carona Sahu Company Ltd. vs Abdul Karim Muna Khan and Others (1994 I LLJ 1100), the Bombay High Court held that as per Section 17–B, full wages last drawn would include wages drawn on the date of termination of service plus yearly increments and dearness allowance. The revision of pay if any, will also have to be taken into account. The same view was held by the Karnataka High Court in Vishvashwaraya Iron & Steel Co. Ltd. vs M. Chandrappa and Another (1993 II LLJ 198) and the Calcutta High Court in Hindustan Wires Ltd. vs Janardan Kundu (1998 I LLJ 542).

A contrary view however, was expressed by the Supreme Court in Dena Bank vs Kirti Kr. T. Patel (1998 I LLJ 1). While reviewing the prior decisions of various judicial bodies it held that the objective of Section 17–B is to relieve to a certain extent, hardship caused to workmen due to delay in implementation of the award. The payment which is required to be made is in the nature of a 'subsistence allowance', which would not be refundable or recoverable from the workman even if the award is set aside by High Court or the Supreme Court. Therefore, the words 'full wages last drawn' must be given their plain and material meaning and they cannot be given the extended meaning as given by the some of the High Courts earlier. This view was confirmed by the Supreme Court in Rajaram Maize Products vs Brij Lal and Another (1999 II LLJ 799).

COMPROMISE PETITIONS

37. *What happens if a compromise petition jointly signed by the chargesheeted employee and the victim (who was assaulted) is arrived at?*

Assault on duty is a serious act of misconduct. Therefore, the enquiry cannot be dispensed with merely because of the receipt of the jointly signed compromise petition. It should form a part of the record of the proceedings and the enquiry should continue since there cannot be compromise with indiscipline. Instances where a complainant is threatened with dire consequences, or coerced by the chargesheeted employee or his men into signing such a compromise petition are common. The enquiry officer need not give any credence to such a petition, unless the punishing authority who instituted the enquiry writes to him not to proceed with the enquiry further.

VICTIMIZATION, UNFAIR LABOUR PRACTICE AND PERVERSE FINDINGS

38. *What do the terms unfair labour practice, victimization and perverse finding mean and what relationship do these concepts have with a disciplinary enquiry?*

Victimization, as a concept in industrial law, has assumed much significance. It is quite usual for a dismissed workman to suggest victimization by the employer for his trade union activities, when all other defence measures fail. In both Hamdard Dawakhana Wakf vs Its Workmen (1962 II LLJ 772 SC) and Bengal Bhatdee Coal Co. Ltd. vs Ram Probesh Singh and Others (1963 I LLJ 291), the Supreme Court held that merely because the workmen were office-bearers or active workers of the union, would by itself be no evidence to prove victimization. Further, in Bharat Bank Limited, Delhi vs Bharat Bank Employees' Union, Delhi (AIR 1950 SC 188) the Supreme Court held as follows:

> The word 'victimization' has not been defined in the statute and is not in any sense a term of law or a term of art. It is an ordinary English word which means that a certain person has become a victim, in other words, that he has been unjustly dealt with.

Victimization therefore, means that a person is a victim of an unfair and arbitrary action. When a person is punished for something he has not done, or because of his trade union activities, or for some other hidden cause, an inference of victimization can be drawn from the quantum of punishment itself. If the employer discriminates against a few with dismissal, though all were guilty of the same charge, this may also amount to an allegation of victimization. In Sengara Singh and Others vs State of Punjab and Others (1984 I LLJ 161), the Supreme Court examined the cases of 1100 members of the police force who were dismissed for participating in a police agitation. Subsequently, the government reinstated a 1000 of them in their original post and withdrew the criminal cases on the recommendation of a review committee. Allowing the appeal in respect of the 100 dismissed members who were not reinstated, the Supreme Court held that:

> All the 1100 dismissed members of the Police Force were guilty of the same misconduct, namely, indiscipline to the same extent and charges as the present appellants. If the indiscipline of a large number of

personnel amongst the dismissed personnel could be condoned or overlooked and after withdrawing the criminal cases against them, they could be reinstated, we see no justification in treating the present appellants differently without pointing out how they were guilty of more serious misconduct, or the degree of indiscipline in their case were higher than compared to those who were reinstated...

This was held to be a denial of equality as guaranteed by Article 14 of the Constitution and the appellants were reinstated. However, in Workmen of Motor Industries Co. Ltd. and Another vs Motor Industries Co. Ltd. (1969 II LLJ 673), the Supreme Court held that if out of a number of workmen, some are found to have taken a leading part in a strike in committing riotous acts, inciting others and assaulting superior officers, there could be no question of victimization and their services were held to be rightly terminated. An act of discrimination calling for intervention of the Court will only occur if among those equally situated, unequal treatment is meted out to one or more of them.

Also, as observed by the Calcutta High Court in National Tobacco Co. of India Ltd. and Others vs Fourth Industrial Tribunal and Others (1960 II LLJ 175), victimization means one of the two things:

(i) the employee was innocent but still has been punished for his trade union activities in acting prejudicially to the interests of the employer or,

(ii) the employee was guilty of the misconduct but the punishment was disproportionate to the misconduct.

Again, in the case of M/s. Hind Construction and Engg. Co. Ltd. vs Their Workmen (AIR 1965 SC 917), it was held that:

Where the punishment is shockingly disproportionate, regard being had to the particular conduct and the past record, or is such that no reasonable employer would ever impose such punishment in like circumstances, the Tribunal would be entitled to treat the imposition of such punishment as itself showing victimization or unfair labour practice.

The distinction between victimization and unfair labour practice is very subtle and sometimes overlaps. In the Industrial Disputes Act, 1947 (as amended in 1982), the Fifth Schedule deals with unfair labour practices (see Annexure 1A). In case victimization is apparent on the face of the record, or in the circumstances of a case, a reversal of the management's decision would be the most likely outcome. In Ashok Kumar vs Union of India and Another (1988, II LLJ 344), the Supreme Court examined a case in which the employee's services were terminated for absence from duty for three days. This punishment was held to be grossly disproportionate to the charge. Setting aside the order of termination of service, the Supreme Court directed the management to enter a punishment of censure in the service record of the employee.

A perverse finding refers to a situation where the enquiry officer holds an employee guilty when, the finding is not based on the evidence, or it is contrary to the evidence adduced. If the finding of the enquiry officer is perverse, the action of the employer based on such finding cannot hold. Hamdard Dawakhana Wakf vs Its Workmen (1962, II LLJ 772 SC).

POWERS OF THE PUNISHING AUTHORITY

39. Can the punishing authority disagree with the findings of the enquiry officer and award immediate punishment?

While the punishing authority may normally agree with the conclusions drawn by the enquiry officer based on the evidence on record, he may also disagree with such a finding in appropriate circumstances. However, if the enquiry officer has given a finding that the charge is not proven, on the same evidence, the punishing authority cannot impose penalty straightaway, unless the finding is perverse. If he does not agree with the findings of the enquiry officer for some valid reason, the punishing authority may order a re-enquiry on the points in issue, so that the chargesheeted employee gets a further opportunity for hearing.

In the case of Thobias vs State of Kerala (1987, II LLJ 504), the Kerala High Court examined a case in which the enquiry officer found the delinquent officer not guilty of the charges. However, the Deputy Inspector General of Police who was the competent authority to punish, did not agree with the findings of the enquiry officer and imposed punishment by withholding two increments of the concerned officer. The delinquent officer was not heard by the Deputy Inspector General of Police before passing the order. The High Court held that his order was bad in law.

As held by the Supreme Court in State of Rajasthan vs M. C. Saxena (1998 I LLJ 1244), the disciplinary authority can disagree with the findings arrived at by the enquiry officer and arrive at his own conclusion. The only requirement is that the said disciplinary authority must record reasons for his disagreement with the findings of the enquiry officer. In that event, the court cannot intervene unless it comes to the conclusion that no reasonable man can reach the said findings.

In Punjab National Bank vs Kunj Bihari Misra and Another (1998 II LLJ 809), the Supreme Court held that when the disciplinary authority disagreed with the findings of the enquiry officer, he has to follow the principles of natural justice. Thus, wherever the disciplinary authority disagrees with the findings of the enquiry officer on a charge, it must record its tentative reasons for such a disagreement and give the delinquent an opportunity to represent himself before the findings are recorded on the charges framed and a final decision of imposing penalty is taken.

Further, as held by the Supreme Court in Bank of India and Another vs Degala Suryanarayana (1999 II LLJ 682), the disciplinary authority may or may not agree with the findings recorded by the enquiry officer. In the case of a disagreement, the disciplinary authority has to record the reasons for the disagreement and then his findings if the evidence available on record is sufficient; or remit the case to the enquiry officer for further enquiry and report. It was also held that the court exercising the jurisdiction of judicial review would not intervene with the findings arrived at in the departmental enquiry proceedings except in a case of mala fide or perversity, i.e., where is there is no evidence to support a finding or where a finding is such that no person acting reasonably and with objectivity could have arrived at that finding.

40. *Since the law requires that only the disciplinary authority or the punishing authority is competent to decide the quantum of punishment after applying his mind to the enquiry proceedings and the findings of the enquiry officer, can any other authority exercise this power? If the disciplinary authority himself happens to be the complainant, or a witness, can he be permitted to perform the role of the punishing authority?*

The law upholds the right of the disciplinary authority or the punishing authority only to take disciplinary action for misconduct. The entire process of disciplinary action from the issue of the chargesheet to the punishment, is within his domain. There are cases reported where action taken by a person subordinate to the punishing authority was set aside in appeal by the courts above, as such a person was not competent to take disciplinary action.

In Steel Authority of India Ltd. Successor of Bokaro Steel Ltd. vs Labour Court and Another (1980 II LLJ 456), the Supreme Court examined whether the chief medical officer who framed the charges against the registration assistant in the Medical Department and constituted the enquiry committee, had the power to do so. It was held that as per Rule 8 read with the Schedule of the Discipline and Appeal Rules of the company, the appointing authority, namely, the personnel manager was the disciplinary authority and as such was the only competent authority to issue the chargesheet and constitute the enquiry committee. Therefore the framing of the chargesheets and the constitution of the enquiry committee by the chief medical officer was without jurisdiction.

In the event the punishing authority happens to be the complainant or a witness, he may have sufficient motivation to be biased. In such a case, it is only proper that the entire proceedings be submitted with the findings of the enquiry officer to an authority who is higher in rank than the punishing authority. In Arjun Chaubey vs Union of India & Others (1984 II LLJ 17), the Supreme Court examined a case in which the main thrust of the charge against the employee related to his conduct against the authority who passed the order of dismissal. The employee (a senior clerk in the office of the Chief Commercial Superintendent, Northern Railway, Varanasi) was issued a chargesheet containing twelve charges including derogatory and offensive behaviour towards the punishing authority—the deputy chief commercial superintendent. On receipt of the explanation, the deputy chief commercial superintendent served a second notice upon the employee to submit a proper explanation to the charges. This was also replied to. Thereafter, the deputy chief commercial superintendent passed an order dismissing the employee on the ground that he was not fit to be retained in service. The Supreme Court held that the punishing authority violated a fundamental principle of natural justice and observed:

> No person can be a judge in his own cause and no witness can certify that his testimony is true. Anyone who has a personal stake in an inquiry must keep himself aloof from the conduct of the inquiry. The order of dismissal passed against the appellant stands vitiated..."

Similarly, in D. J. Warkari vs K. V. Karanjikar (1980 II LLJ 270), the division bench of the Bombay High Court held that when the disciplinary authority was a witness to a theft, his decision as punishing authority would be biased and amount to an empty formality.

41. *It has been established that an enquiry officer plays a key role in conducting a fair and proper disciplinary enquiry. Can an enquiry officer, who is part of the industrial organization, be entrusted with conducting the disciplinary enquiry, if he was also associated with the preliminary enquiry?*

The role and responsibilities of an enquiry officer have been discussed indepth earlier. He is entrusted to conduct the enquiry, a quasi-judicial function, in accordance to the principles of natural justice because the management believes that he can conduct an impartial enquiry without prejudice, and would give a reasonable opportunity to the chargesheeted employee to defend himself. Although only a person who is acquainted with the procedure and the law on the subject can perform this task effectively, there is no bar in appointing an outside lawyer who has no interest in the outcome, to conduct the enquiry of a chargesheet Saran Motors Pvt. Ltd. vs Viswanath (1963 II LLJ 396 SC); Indian Telephone Industries Ltd. vs D. K. Shukla (2000 1 LLJ 531). It cannot however, be entrusted to the person who had conducted the preliminary enquiry based upon which the chargesheet was issued. Such a person can only appear and depose as a management witness, if the management wishes to rely on the preliminary enquiry statements, during the enquiry.

In Jayadevan and Others vs Commandant, MSP and Others (1984 I LLJ 521), the Kerala High Court examined the question of the validity of an officer conducting the preliminary enquiry and also the regular enquiry. It was held that:

> It is impossible to think that the author of the preliminary report could thereafter have kept an open mind about the pertinent questions which would arise for consideration in the subsequent formal enquiry which was yet to be held.

Setting aside the order of removal from service of the petitioner, the court observed in this case that 'reasonable opportunity in the real sense of the expression was a casualty'.

Also, in Sreeramulu vs State (AIR 1970 114), the Andhra Pradesh High Court observed:

> ... there can be no doubt that certain basic principles of natural justice apply equally to administrative enquiries as to judicial enquiries. A person who has conducted a preliminary enquiry and found a *prima facie* case for a regular enquiry, will not be permitted to conduct regular enquiry because he has already in some way formed an opinion in the case or where an administrative superior has expressed definite view on the conduct of a delinquent officer, he will not be permitted to hold an enquiry.

Since in a domestic enquiry the question of prejudice, bias, etc., of the enquiry officer is often raised, a person who had conducted the preliminary enquiry should not be appointed to conduct the subsequent formal enquiry. Therefore, as observed by the Supreme

Court in the case of Associated Cement Companies Ltd. vs Their Workmen and Another (1963 II LLJ 396), it is desirable that the conduct of domestic enquiries should be left to such officers of the employer who are not likely to import their personal knowledge into the proceedings which they are holding as enquiry officers.

DISCHARGE SIMPLICITER

42. *In some standing orders/service rules, there is a provision for termination of service by the employer by giving one or three months' notice to the employee or paying him salary in lieu thereof. Does this imply that the employer can terminate the services of an employee at any time and without any reason?*

While a company's standing orders/service rules contain the terms and conditions of employment, an employer is not free to exercise this right arbitrarily in terminating the services of any employee. In 1965, the Industrial Disputes Act, 1947, was amended and Section 2–A was added. According to this provision, any workman whose services have been terminated by the employer can challenge the decision by raising an industrial dispute without the support of the trade union or any other workmen. Once such a dispute is referred to a labour court/tribunal, the employer's decision may not succeed and the workman may be reinstated with other consequential benefits for the past period.

This provision has been repeatedly challenged in various judicial forums. The apex court has given its verdict in favour of the workman, whether the termination was as a result of 'loss of confidence', or otherwise. In Uptron India Ltd. vs Shammi Bhan and Another (1998 I LLJ 1165), the Supreme Court examined the validity of termination of service as per Cl 17(g) of the certified standing orders of the company whereby 'the services of a workman are liable to automatic termination if he overstays on leave without permission for more than seven days. In case of sickness, the medical certificate must be submitted within a week'.

The Supreme Court referring to earlier decisions on the subject, held that the conferment of 'permanent' status of an employee guarantees security of tenure. It is now well settled that the services of a permanent employee, whether employed by the Government, government company, statutory corporation or any other authority as per Article 12, cannot be terminated abruptly and arbitrarily, either by giving a month's or three months' notice, or pay in lieu thereof, or even without notice, notwithstanding that there may be a stipulation to that effect either in the contract of service or in the certified standing orders. The provision of Section 17(g) of the certified standing orders cannot withstand judicial scrutiny as it is incompatible with the notion of social justice, as there is no statutory protection available to the workmen. The contract of service is often unilateral in character and as such an agreement between two unequals. The case law was reviewed earlier by the Constitution Bench in Delhi Transport Corporation vs DTC Mazdoor Congress and Others (1991 I LLJ 395). The majority of judges reiterated the earlier view that the services of a confirmed employee could not be legally terminated by a simple notice. This being the legal position, the action taken against the permanent employee, was illegal.

Further, in D. K. Yadav vs J. M. A. Industries Ltd. (1993 II LLJ 696), the Supreme Court reviewed a case of summary termination of service of the appellant for unauthorized absence without any enquiry as per Clause 13 (2)(iv) of the certified standing order. The provision of loss of lien as per this clause was held to be arbitrary, unjust and unfair, violating Article 14 of the Constitution as it was contrary to the principles of natural justice. The Supreme Court also held that the right to life enshrined in Article 21 of the Constitution would include the right to livelihood. The order of termination has the implication of jeopardizing not only the worker's livelihood but also of their dependants. Therefore, before taking any action of putting an end to the tenure of an employee, fair play requires that a reasonable opportunity be given and domestic enquiry conducted, complying with the principles of natural justice. The order of termination of service of the employee was set aside and the management was directed to reinstate the employee and pay him back wages.

In view of the current legal position, it has been held by the Supreme Court in Uptron India's case (1998 I LLJ 1165) that:

> any clause in the Certified Standing Orders providing for automatic termination of service of a permanent employee, not directly related to "Production" in a factory or Industrial Establishment, would be bad if it does not purport to provide an opportunity of hearing to the employee whose services are treated to have come to an end automatically.

TERMINATION OF SERVICE OF A PROBATIONER

43. *A person appointed on probation cannot claim permanency in employment unless his performance is satisfactory during the probationary period. In some companies in the appointment letter there is a clause that his services can be terminated at any time during the period of probation or thereafter, without assigning any reason. What is the legal position on this subject?*

A probationer does not have any right to automatic permanency on the expiry of the probationary period, unless specified by the company's rules. This issue has been dealt with in a number of the cases by the

Supreme Court. It has been held that a probationer's service can be terminated during the probationary period if he commits an act of misconduct as per the company's standing orders, for which even a permanent employee can be punished Management of Express Newspaper (P) Ltd. vs Presiding Officer, Labour Court, Madurai (AIR 1964 SC 806). His services cannot however, be terminated during the probationary period on the grounds of lack of performance.

In V. P. Ahuja vs State of Punjab & Others (2000 I LLJ 1099), the Supreme Court held that a probationer, like a temporary servant, is also entitled to certain protection and his services cannot be terminated arbitrarily, or in a punitive manner without complying with the principles of natural justice as it is stigmatic. The order is founded on the ground that the applicant had failed in the performance of his duties administratively and technically. In Dipti Prakash Banerjee vs Satyendra Nath Bose National Centre for Basic Sciences, Calcutta & Others (1999 1 LLJ 1054), the Supreme Court discussed all prior cases of termination of service during the probationary period and provided detailed guidelines about the circumstances in which the termination of services of a probationer can be said to be founded on misconduct and the meaning of the expression 'stigma'.

In this connection, reference may also be made to the decisions in respect of the following three cases. (a) Agra Electric Supply Company vs Alladin (1969 II LLJ 540 SC); (b) Management of Brooke Bond India (P) Ltd. vs Y. K. Goutam (1973 II LLJ 454 SC); and (c) Biswajit Deb Roy vs Indian Overseas Bank and Others (1987 II LLJ 288 Calcutta).

However, in cases where the concerned employee is a workman under the Industrial Disputes Act, and if during the probationary period he has completed 240 days in the period of the last twelve months, 'conditions precedent to retrenchment of workmen' as per the Act must be followed before termination of service of the probationer Mohan Lal vs Bharat Electronics Ltd.(1981 II LLJ 70 SC).

RESIGNATION AND ITS WITHDRAWAL

44. *In the event an employee submits his resignation with due notice, can the employer accept it before the expiry of the notice period by waiving the notice period? What happens if the employee writes to the employer requesting for withdrawal of the resignation before the expiry of the notice period?*

Just as an employer is entitled to terminate the services of an employee as per the contract of employment/ service rules/standing orders, by giving notice or paying wages in lieu of the notice period, the employee can also terminate the appointment by submitting his resignation with notice. The period of notice on either side normally varies between one and three months. Sometimes, an employee after submitting his resignation with notice, may withdraw the same during the notice period. An employer cannot object to this, even if the resignation has already been accepted, waiving the notice period. However, there have been instances where the employers refused to allow the concerned employees to withdraw their resignation and insisted that they had been released from service, resulting in litigation. Some decisions on this point are given below.

In Punjab National Bank vs Mr. P. K. Mittal (1989 I LLJ 368 SC), an officer sent a letter of resignation as per Regulation 20(2) of the Punjab National Bank (Officers) Service Regulations, 1979, to be effective after three months' notice period. The bank sent a letter to the officer within 17 days of the date of resignation stating that it was accepted, waiving the notice period. This decision was challenged by the officer by filing a writ petition before the High Court praying for a direction to treat him in service during the notice period. The officer withdrew his resignation during the pendency of the writ petition but before the period of notice of three months was over. The High Court held that the officer's resignation was to be effective only after expiry of three months' notice and he had a right to withdraw the resignation before this period.

The bank filed an appeal by special leave to the Supreme Court against the order of the High Court. The Supreme Court held that resignation is a voluntary act of an employee and an employer does not have the power to accept the resignation with immediate effect against the employees' wishes, even though the notice is only of a future resignation. This would amount to forcing a date of termination on the employee other than the one he is entitled to choose under the regulations. The employee can withdraw his resignation before the resignation becomes effective. In this case, the resignation stood withdrawn and the employee continued to be in service. A similar view was taken by the Supreme Court in Union of India vs Gopal Chandra Mishra and Others (AIR 1978 SC 694).

A similar case, P. Nagaraju vs State of Karnataka and Others (1985 II LLJ 96), came up for consideration before the High Court of Karnataka at Bangalore. In this case, a clerk in the service of M/s Kushalnagar Works at Kudige tendered his resignation with a month's notice on August 23, 1969 effective from September 22, 1969. The manager conveyed his decision accepting the resignation on the same day, to be effective from September 22, 1969. Subsequently, the party made a representation to the managing director on September 3, 1969 withdrawing his resignation. However, he was not allowed to continue in service on the ground that his resignation had already been accepted as per the order dated August 23, 1969. He was relieved from his duties with effect from September 22, 1969. The party raised an industrial dispute which was referred to the Labour Court, Mysore for adjudication. The Labour Court decided the reference in favour of the management. Aggrieved by the order of the Labour Court, the party filed a writ petition. Allowing the writ petition, the High Court held that:

> Where the resignation tendered is to become effective with effect from a future date, the employee who has tendered resignation has a right to withdraw the resignation before it becomes effective and he goes out of employment. In the withdrawal of prospective resignation, the employee is entitled to continue in service as if he had not tendered resignation, as there was no resignation to be acted upon.

Voluntary Retirement and Withdrawal

45. *If an employee submits an application for voluntary retirement effective from a particular date, can the employer accept the request before the expiry of the period? In the event employee wants to withdraw the application for voluntary retirement before its expiry date, does this have to be accepted?*

Voluntary retirement, as the name indicates, is *voluntary* in nature on the part of the employee. This decision is normally taken, in the given circumstances, without any persuasion or pressure. A request for voluntary retirement is like resignation and it can be withdrawn inspite of acceptance by employer before its effective date. As held by the Supreme Court in (a) Balram Gupta vs Union of India (1987 II LLJ 541) and in (b) Sambhu Murari Sinha vs Project Development India and Another (2000 II LLJ 935), it is now well settled that even if the voluntary retirement notice is requested by an employee and is accepted by the authority within the time indicated, the employee has the right to withdraw the proposal before the date of retirement is reached.

In J. N. Srivastava vs Union of India and Another (1999 I LLJ 546 SC), an employee submitted an application for voluntary retirement with the notice period of three months. His application was accepted. However, before the expiry of the period, he gave a notice for withdrawal of the voluntary retirement application which was turned down. In this case the Supreme Court held that it cannot be said that the appellant had no *locus standi* to withdraw his proposal for voluntary retirement before the expiry of the three months period. The employer refused to act on the request for withdrawal and the appellant was forced to hand over charge on the expiry of the period. The Supreme Court allowed the appeal and directed the respondent to treat the request for withdrawal of voluntary retirement as valid. The net result of this order was that the appellant was treated to be in service till the date of his superannuation when he completed 58 years of age.

POWERS OF A CIVIL COURT

46. *Under Section 2–A of the Industrial Disputes Act, 1947, a workman can challenge the order of dismissal, discharge, retrenchment or otherwise termination of his service. Can he also approach a civil court for redressal against the order of his dismissal? What is the remedy for those who are not covered by the Act?*

The protection under Section 2–A of the Act has been available to an individual workman since December, 1965, to challenge the order of dismissal, discharge, etc., as specified. Thus, there is no need for him to go to any other forum like a civil court which although has the power to declare dismissals wrongful in appropriate cases of breach of contract, can only award damages but not the relief of reinstatement in service. As held by the Supreme Court in Sirsi Municipality by its President, Sirsi vs Cecliakom Francis Tellis (AIR 1973, SC 855):

> The cases of dismissal of a servant fall under three broad heads. The first head relates to relationship of master and servant governed purely by contract of employment. Any breach of contract in such a case is enforced by a suit for wrongful dismissal and damages. Just as a contract of employment is not capable of specific performance, similarly, breach of contract of employment is not capable of finding a declaratory judgement of subsistence of employment. A declaration of unlawful termination and restoration to service in such a case of contract of employment would be indirectly an instance of specific performance of contract for personal services. Such a declaration is not permissible under the law of Specific Relief Act.
>
> The second type of cases of master and servant arises under industrial law. Under that breach of law, a servant who is wrongfully dismissed may be reinstated. This is a special provision under industrial law. This relief is a departure from the relief available under the Indian Contract Act and the Specific Relief Act which do not provide reinstatement of a servant.
>
> The third category of cases of master and servant arises in regard to the servant in employment of the State or of other Public or Local Authorities or bodies created under statute.
>
> Termination or dismissal of what is described as a pure contract of master and servant is not declared to be a nullity, however illegal it may be. The reason is that dismissal in breach of contract is remedied by damages. In the case of the servant

of the State or the local authorities or statutory bodies, courts have declared in appropriate cases the dismissal to be invalid if the dismissal is contrary to the rules of natural justice or if the dismissal is in violation of the provisions of the statute...

The courts keep the States and the Public authorities within the limits of their statutory power. Where a State or a public authority dismisses an employee in violation of the mandatory procedural requirements or on grounds which are not sanctioned or supported by statute, the courts may exercise jurisdiction to declare the act of dismissal to be a nullity. Such implication of public employment is thus distinguished from private employment in pure cases of master and servant.

In S. R. Tewari vs District Board, Agra (1964 I LLJ 1), the Supreme Court observed that dismissal or removal of an officer/servant might be effected under the rules only after giving a reasonable opportunity of showing cause against the action proposed to be taken. It held that a dismissed employee might in an appropriate case, obtain a declaratory judgement that the dismissal was wrongful in three cases. These are: (*a*) in the case of public servants covered under Article 311 (2) of the Constitution; (*b*) in cases covered under the industrial law; and (*c*) cases where the act of statutory bodies are in breach of mandatory obligations imposed by a statute. It is clear that the above categories exclude those who are in private employment but are outside the scope of the Industrial Disputes Act. They are to be governed only by their contract of employment with the employer. The Supreme Court while examining whether the validity of termination of service of a lecturer by the managing committee of an associated college can be challenged in a writ petition under Article 226 of the Constitution in Vidya Ram

Mishra vs Managing Committee, Sri Jai Narain College (1972 I LLJ 442), observed as follows:

> It is well-settled that when there is a purported termination of contract of service, a declaration that the contact of service still subsisted would not be made in the absence of special circumstances, because of the principle that Courts do not ordinarily enforce specific performance of contracts of service. If the master rightfully ends the contract, there can be no complaint. If the master wrongfully ends the contract, then the servant can pursue a claim for damages. So, even if the master wrongfully dismisses the servant in breach of the contract, the employment is effectively terminated. [See (*a*) Executive Committee UP State Warehousing Corporation Ltd. vs Chandra Kiran Tyagi (1970 I LLJ 32 SC) (*b*) Indian Airlines Corporation vs Sukhdeo Rai (1971 (23) FLR 1) (*c*) Sitaram Kashiram Konda vs Pigment Cakes and Chemicals Manf. Co., (1979 II LLJ 444 SC) and (*d*) Premier Automobiles Ltd. vs K. S. Wadke and Others (1975 II LLJ 445 SC)].

Therefore this implies that those employees who are covered only by the law of master and servant cannot demand reinstatement, even if wrongfully dismissed in violation of the principles of natural justice and the contract of employment. For them, the only remedy is to file a suit before a civil court claiming damages for wrongful dismissal from service. The same analogy is however, not applicable in the three instances referred to above where the courts can declare that the contract of service still existed even when there is a termination of contract of service by the employer. Thus, the court can declare as follows in appropriate cases:

> ...that a public servant who is dismissed from service in contravention of Art. 311 continues to remain in service, even though by doing so, the State is in effect forced to employ the servant whom it

does not desire to employ. Similarly, under the industrial law, jurisdiction of labour court and industral tribunal to compel the employer to employ a workman, whom he does not desire to employ, is recognized. The Courts are also invested with the power to declare invalid the act of a statutory body, if by doing the act, the body has acted in breach of mandatory obligation imposed by the statute, even if by making the declaration the body is compelled to do something which it does not desire to do (S. R. Tewari's case: 1964 I LLJ 1 SC).

Many decisions on the rights and obligations of employers relating to the dismissal/termination of services of their workmen covered under the Industrial Disputes Act, 1947, have been discussed. A number of decisions relating to employees of public corporations that are instrumentalities of the government and statutory bodies, who were dismissed or whose services were terminated, have also been discussed. In both cases, the decisions of the employer were put to an acid test—whether there was any violation of the principles of natural justice, or statutory rules or regulations, or in the matter of their right to a hearing, and sometimes, the validity of the rule itself, as in the case of the Steel Authority of India Ltd. and Another vs Dilip Kumar Debnath (1989 I LLJ 133 SC). In this case, the employer was considered to be a State under Article 12 of the Constitution and the employees were thus entitled to the protection of Article 14 and Article 16 of the Constitution. It has been held by the Supreme Court that even temporary government employees enjoy the protection of Article 311 (2) in case of penal orders Kanhailal vs Dist. Judge and Others (AIR 1983 SC 351).

The jurisdication of a civil court on industrial matters came up for review by the Supreme Court in the case of Premier Automobiles Ltd. vs K. S. Wadke (1975 II LLJ 445). The Court held as follows:

(1) If the dispute is not an industrial dispute, nor does it relate to enforcement of any right under the Act, the remedy lies in the-Civil Court.

(2) If the dispute is an industrial dispute arising out of a right or liability under the general or common law and not under the Act, the jurisdiction of Civil Court is alternative leaving it to the election of the suitor concerned to choose his remedy for the relief which is competent to be granted a particular remedy.

(3) If the industrial dispute relates to the enforcement of a right or an obligation created under the Act, then the only remedy available to the suitor is to get an adjudication done under the Act.

(4) If the right which is sought to be enforced is created under the Act such as Chapter V–A, then the remedy for its enforcement is either Sec. 33C, or the raising of an industrial dispute, as the case may be.

We may, however, in relation to principle No. 2 stated above hasten to add that there will hardly be a dispute which will be an industrial dispute within the meaning of Sec. 2(k) of the Act and yet will be one arising out of a right or liability under the general or *common law* only and not under the Act. Such a contingency, for example, may arise in regard to the dismissal of an unsponsored workman which in view of the provision of law contained in Sec. 2–A of the Act, will be an industrial dispute even though it may otherwise be an individual dispute.

Civil Courts will, therefore, hardly have any occasion to deal with the type of cases falling under principle No. 2. Cases of industrial dispute, by and large invariably, are bound to be covered by principle No. 3 stated above.

In Jitendra Nath Biswas vs Empire of India & Ceylon Tea Company and Another (1989 I LLJ 572), the Supreme Court held that the scheme of the Industrial

Disputes Act clearly excludes the jurisdiction of the civil court by implication in respect of remedies which are available under the Act and for which a complete procedure and machinery has been provided therein. Further, in Rajasthan State Road Transport Corporation and Another vs Krishnakant (1995 II LLJ 728), the Supreme Court summarized the principles applicable to the jurisdiction of a civil court in relation to the Industrial Disputes Act as follows:

(1) Where the dispute arises from general law of contract. i.e. where reliefs are claimed on the basis of the general law of contract, a suit filed in civil court cannot be said to be not maintainable, even though such a dispute may also constitute an "industrial dispute" within the meaning of Section 2(k) or Section 2–A of the Industrial Disputes Act, 1947.

(2) Where, however, the dispute involves recognition, observance or enforcement of any of the rights or obligations created by the Industrial Disputes Act, the only remedy is to approach the forums created by the said Act.

(3) Similarly, where the dispute involves the recognition, observance or enforcement of rights and obligations created by enactments like Industrial Employment (Standing Orders) Act, 1946 which can be called "sister enactments" to Industrial Disputes Act and which do not provide a forum for resolution of such disputes, the only remedy shall be to approach the forums created by the Industrial Disputes Act provided they constitute industrial disputes within the meaning of Section 2(k) and Section 2–A of Industrial Disputes Act or where such enactment says that such dispute shall be either treated as an industrial dispute or says that it shall be adjudicated by any of the forums created by the Industrial Dispute Act. Otherwise, recourse to Civil Court is open.

(4) It is not correct to say that the remedies provided by the Industrial Disputes Act are not equally effective for the reason that access to the forum depends upon a reference being made by the appropriate government. The power to make a reference conferred upon the government is to be exercised to effectuate the object of the enactment and hence not unguided. The rule is to make a reference unless, of course, the dispute raised is a toally frivolous one *ex-facie*. The power conferred is the power to refer and not the power to decide, though it may be that the government is entitled to examine whether the dispute is *ex-facie* frivolous, not meriting an adjudication.

(5) Consistent with the policy of law aforesaid, we commend to the parliament and the State Legislatures to make a provision enabling a workman to approach the Labour Court/Industrial Tribunal directly—i.e., without the requirement of a reference by the Government—in case of industrial disputes covered by Section 2–A of the Industrial Disputes Act. This would go a long way in removing the misgivings with respect to the effectiveness of the remedies provided by the Industrial Disputes Act.

(6) The certified Standing Orders framed under and in accordance with the Industrial Employment (Standing Orders) Act, 1946 are statutorily imposed conditions of service and are binding both upon the employers and employees, though they do not amount to "statutory provisions". Any violation of these Standing Orders entitles an employee to appropriate relief either before the forums created by the Industrial Disputes Act or the Civil Court where recourse to Civil Court is open according to the principles indicated herein.

(7) The policy of law emerging from Industrial Disputes Act and its sister enactments is to provide

an alternative dispute resolution mechanism to the workmen, a mechanism which is speedy, inexpensive, inforxmal and unencumbered by the plethora of procedural laws and appeal, upon appeals and revisions applicable to civil courts. Indeed, the powers of the Courts and Tribunals under the Industrial Disputes Act are far more extensive in the sense that they can grant such relief as they think appropriate in the circumstances for putting an end to industrial dispute.

It is therefore, clear that a civil court cannot entertain a dispute between an employer and a workman if it falls under Section 2(k) or 2–A of the Industrial Disputes Act. Such a dispute must be adjudicated in the forum created under the Industrial Dispute Act alone.

TIME LIMIT FOR RAISING AN INDUSTRIAL DISPUTE

47. *There have been instances where a workman dismissed or discharged for misconduct raised an industrial dispute after a lapse of several years, and the management has found it difficult to locate the relevant records relating to his dismissal/discharge. Should there be some legal restriction on challenging the management's order of discharge/dismissal/termination as exists in the Shops and Establishments Acts of some States?*

In Ajaib Singh vs Sirhind Co-op Marketing-cum-Processing Service Society Ltd. and Another (1999 1 LLJ 1260), there was delay of approximately seven years in raising an industrial dispute. It was held by the Supreme Court that the provisions of Article 137 of the Schedule to the Limitation Act, 1963, are not applicable to proceedings under the Industrial Disputes Act. If the order of the dismissal is challenged belatedly, the dispute would still continue for adjudication and the only question would be whether to deprive back wages for the period of delay in raising such a dispute if on merits it is to succeed. Again in Mahavir Singh vs U. P. State Electricity Board and Others (1999 II LLJ 482), the Supreme Court allowed the appeal of the appellant *chowkidar* who raised an industrial dispute after more than seven years from the date of his termination. The Supreme Court restored the order of the Labour Court reinstating him, although the High Court took the view that as the dispute was raised belatedly, the reference itself was incompetent, though it agreed with the Labour Court that on merits the termination order could not be sustained and was illegal. Also, in the case of Gurmail Singh vs Principal, Government College of Education and Others (2000 I LLJ 1080), the Supreme Court held that the delay of about eight years in the raising of an industrial dispute questioning termination would not wipe out the dispute.

However, in State Bank of Indore vs Gobindrao (1997 I LLJ 841), the Supreme Court allowed the appeal by the State Bank of Indore and held that the writ filed by Sri Govindrao under Article 226 of the Constitution was a delayed one and it should not have been entertained by the High Court. In this case, the employee was dismissed from service on October 3, 1977 whereas the writ petition was filed on April 6, 1987. Thus, the Supreme Court held that in the matter of a writ under Article 226 of the Constitution, such delays cannot be condoned.

SOLITARY WITNESS

48. *Can an employee be punished only on the evidence of a solitary witness?*

In Banaras Electric Light and Power Co. Ltd. vs Labour Court II Lucknow (1972, II LLJ 328), the Supreme Court held that:

There is no rule of evidence which lays down that the evidence of a solitary witness cannot be relied upon or merely because there is a solitary witness in support of the charge, no conclusion can be based upon it even though the evidence of that witness is acceptable as true.

Depending on the facts and circumstances of a case, normally, before concluding that a charge is established, corroborative evidence is necessary. The charge should not be accepted as proven unless every possibility of getting the evidence corroborated by another witness has been explored. However, if in the circumstances of the case, this is not possible, in the event another person was not supposed to be in the vicinity, one man's version against the other can be accepted to prove a fact under certain circumstances. For example, when the assistant manager of a coal mine while inspecting a remote site underground, was abused when he asked the only workman present why he was sleeping on duty, his evidence was accepted in support of the charge as there was no allegation of personal bias or enmity against the complainant. The principle is that where the evidence is highly probative, the same can be accepted without corroboration but with reasons for the same.

COMPENSATION IN LIEU OF REINSTATEMENT

49. *In previous cases, the Supreme Court has sometimes awarded Rs. 200,000 or more as compensation for wrongful termination of service. Did the employer take action against those in the management who were responsible for such lapses?*

In several cases that were pending for a long time, the Supreme Court awarded compensation in lieu of reinstatement of the concerned employees. In the case of

Chandulal vs Management of PanAm Airways (1985 II LLJ 181), the amount was Rs. 200,000. In Santraj and Another vs O. P. Singla and Another (1984 II LLJ 19 SC), an amount of Rs. 200,000 to each of the two workmen was awarded to cover back wages and compensation in lieu of reinstatement. In Sudersan Motors (P) Ltd. vs Ameerjan and Another (1984 II LLJ 22 SC), Rs. 225,000 was awarded under similar circumstances. Also, in the case of K. C. Joshi vs Union of India and Others (1985 II LLJ 416 SC), an amount of Rs. 200,000 was ordered to be paid as compensation in lieu of reinstatement and back wages.

Although there is no record whether the concerned employers took any action against the relevant management personnel for such lapses, no employer can be expected to view such matters kindly.

THE PRESENT SCENARIO

50. After the discussion so far, any private employer who wishes to discipline a delinquent workman will wonder whether it is safe to dismiss a workman, even in a case in which misconduct has been established in a domestic enquiry held for that purpose. Is there any guarantee that the employer's action will be upheld by the courts as valid? At present, in most cases decided by the labour court/tribunal, the decisions go in favour of the workmen and are upheld in appeal. Section 17–B of the Industrial Disputes Act, protects a workman even more by providing for payment of full wages last drawn to the workman who has been ordered to be reinstated. In the face of these restrictions, how is it possible to maintain discipline in industry, which is so important for the very existence of an industrial unit?

Indiscipline exists and is growing in many areas. It is a fact that in a majority of cases, decisions of the management relating to dismissal are reversed by the labour court/tribunal. It is also true, that more often than not the decisions of the High Courts or the Supreme Court are in favour of the employee. Due to growing indiscipline among workers, many industrial units have lost their economic viability and become sick, quite a few have had no choice a number among them have but to close down, leaving hundreds of employees out of jobs. If the causes of indiscipline in industry are analyzed, the findings may reveal that employers, trade unions as well as government policy are all responsible for this lamentable state of affairs.

Workers in India by and large, are not too ambitious and all they want is security of employment. In the present large scale unemployment scenario, the loss of a job is critical. Inflation ensures that even with a full month's wages, employees find it difficult to make both ends meet. This is one reason why workers these days are reluctant to respond to even a single day's strike called by the unions, though due to other compulsions they cannot oppose these strikes. If employees could be guaranteed fair treatment and support from their employer and an assurance that they would not be unjustly treated, victimized or discriminated against, many of them might not join any trade union for protection, nor would they need the unions' support to raise an industrial dispute under Section 2–A of the Industrial Disputes Act.

The question that arises at this juncture is whether or not the management is prepared to change its styles of managing conflict and disciplinary situations. Is it prepared to scale down from its position of strength, compromise some of its prerogatives and help create an atmosphere free from strife and mistrust? Once the management is able to establish its credibility with regard to fair play and justice, it may find fewer problems of indiscipline. For creating such a work culture, the management must take the initiative with conviction. This is not an easy process and obstacles will be plenty. However, if the management is determined towards creating a platform of mutual cooperation, both sides would soon realize that it is in their mutual interest to establish a proper forum for resolution of conflicts through negotiation.

However, to what extent this will succeed would depend largely upon the character, conviction and calibre of those who are entrusted with the responsibility of leadership, both in the management, as well as the trade unions.

The Industrial Disputes Act, 1947
Relevant Excerpts

DEFINITIONS

SECTION 2

(oo) "retrenchment" means the termination by the employer of the service of a workman for any reason whatsoever, otherwise than as a punishment inflicted by way of disciplinary action, but does not include:

(a) voluntary retirement of the workman; or

(b) retirement of the workman on reaching the age of superannuation if the contract of employment between the employer and the workman concerned contains a stipulation in that behalf; or

(bb) termination of the service of the workman as a result of the non-renewal of the contract of employment between the employer and the workman concerned on its expiry or of such contract being terminated under a stipulation in that behalf contained therein; or

(c) termination of the service of a workman on the ground of continued ill-health.

(rr) "wages" means all remuneration capable of being expressed in terms of money, which would, if the terms of employment, expressed or implied were fulfilled, be payable to a workman in respect of his employment, or of work done in such employment, and includes-

(i)   such allowances (including dearness allowance) as the workman is for the time being entitled to;

(ii)   the value of any house accommodation, or of supply of light, water, medical attendance or other amenity or of any service or of any concessional supply of foodgrains or other articles;

(iii)   any travelling concessions;

(iv)   any commission payable on the promotion of sales or business or both;

but does not include-

(a)   any bonus;

(b)   any contribution paid or payable by the employer to any pension fund or provident fund or for the benefit of the workman under any law for the time being in force;

(c)   any gratuity payable on the termination of his service;

(S)   "workman" means any person (including an apprentice) employed in any industry to do any manual, unskilled, skilled, technical, operational, clerical or supervisory work for hire or reward, whether the terms of employment be express or implied, and for the purposes of any proceeding under this Act in relation to an industrial dispute, includes any such person who has been dismissed, discharged or retrenched in connection with, or as a consequence of, that dispute, but does not include any such person:

(i)   who is subject to the Air Force Act, 1950 (45 of 1950), or the Army Act, 1950 (46 of 1950), or the Navy Act, 1957 (62 of 1957); or

(ii)   who is employed in the police service or as an officer or other employee of a prison; or

(iii)   who is employed mainly in a managerial or administrative capacity; or

(iv) who, being employed in a supervisory capacity, draws wages exceeding one thousand six hundred rupees per mensem or exercises, either by the nature of the duties attached to the office or by reason of the powers vested in him, functions mainly of a managerial nature.

SECTION 2-A : DISMISSAL ETC. OF AN INDIVIDUAL WORKMAN TO BE DEEMED TO BE AN INDUSTRIAL DISPUTE

Where any employer discharges, dismisses, retrenches or otherwise terminates the services of an individual workman, any dispute or difference between that workman and his employer connected with, or arising out of, such discharge, dismissal, retrenchment or termination shall be deemed to be an industrial dispute notwithstanding that no other workman nor any union of workmen is a party to the dispute.

SECTION 10(2A): REFERENCE OF DISPUTES TO BOARDS, COURTS OR TRIBUNALS

An order referring an industrial dispute to a Labour Court, Tribunal or National Tribunal under this section shall specify the period within which such Labour Court, Tribunal or National Tribunal shall submit its award on such dispute to the appropriate Government:

Provided that where such industrial dispute is connected with an individual workman, no such period shall exceed three months:

Provided further that where the parties to an industrial dispute apply in the prescribed manner, whether jointly or separately, to the Labour Court, Tribunal or National Tribunal for extension of such period or for any other reason, and the presiding officer of such Labour Court, Tribunal or National Tribunal considers it necessary or expedient to extend such period, he may, for reasons to be recorded in writing, extend such period by such further period as he may think fit:

Provided also that in computing any period specified in this sub-section, the period, if any, for which the proceedings before the Labour Court, Tribunal or National Tribunal had been stayed by any injunction or order of a Civil Court shall be excluded:

Provided also that no proceedings before a Labour Court, Tribunal or National Tribunal shall lapse merely on the ground that any period specified under this sub-section had expired without such proceedings being completed.

SECTION 11(4): PROCEDURE AND POWERS OF CONCILIATION OFFICER, BOARDS, COURTS AND TRIBUNALS

A Conciliation Officer may enforce the attendance of any person for the purpose of examining of such person or call for and inspect any document which he has ground for considering to be relevant to the industrial dispute or to be necessary for the purpose of verifying the implementation of any award or carrying out any other duty imposed on him under this Act, and for the aforesaid purposes, the conciliation officer shall have the same powers as are vested in a Civil Court under the Code of Civil Procedure, 1908 (5 of 1908), in respect of enforcing the attendance of any person and examining him or of compelling the production of documents.

SECTION 11–A: POWERS OF LABOUR COURTS, TRIBUNALS AND NATIONAL TRIBUNALS TO GIVE APPROPRIATE RELIEF IN A CASE OF DISCHARGE OR DISMISSAL OF WORKMEN

Where an industrial dispute relating to the discharge or dismissal of a workman has been referred to a Labour Court, Tribunal or National Tribunal for adjudication, and in the course of the adjudication proceedings, the Labour Court, Tribunal or National Tribunal, as the case may be, is satisfied that the order of discharge or dismissal was not justified, it may, by its award, set aside the order of discharge or dismissal and direct reinstatement of the workman on such terms and conditions, if any, as it thinks fit, or give such other relief to the workman including the award of any lesser punishment in lieu of discharge or dismissal as the circumstances of the case may require:

Provided that in any proceeding under this section, the Labour Court, Tribunal or National Tribunal, as the case may be, shall rely only on the materials on record and shall not take any fresh evidence in relation to the matter.

SECTION 17B: PAYMENT OF FULL WAGES TO WORKMAN PENDING PROCEEDINGS IN HIGHER COURTS

Where in any case, a Labour Court, Tribunal or National Tribunal by its award directs reinstatement of any workman and the employer prefers any proceedings against such award in a High Court or the Supreme Court, the employer shall be liable to pay such workman, during the period of pendency of such proceedings in the High Court or the Supreme Court, full wages last drawn by him, inclusive of any maintenance allowance admissible to him under any rule if the workman had not been employed in any establishment during such period and an affidavit by such workman had been filed to that effect in such Court:

Provided that where it is proved to the satisfaction of the High Court or the Supreme Court that such workman had been employed and had been receiving adequate remuneration during any such period or part thereof, the court shall order that no wages shall be payable under this section for such period or part, as the case may be.

SECTION 25F: CONDITIONS PRECEDENT TO RETRENCHMENT OF WORKMEN

No workman employed in any industry who has been in continuous service for not less than one year under an employer shall be retrenched by that employer until:

(a) the workman has been given one month's notice in writing indicating the reasons for retrenchment and the period of notice has expired, or the workman has been paid, in lieu of such notice, wages for the period of the notice;

(b) the workman has been paid, at the time of retrenchment, compensation which shall be equivalent to fifteen days' average pay for every completed year of continuous service or any part thereof in excess of six months; and

(c) notice in the prescribed manner is served on the appropriate Government or such authority as may be specified by the appropriate Government by notification in the Official Gazette.

Note: The provisions of Sec. 25F apply to industrial establishments to which provisions of Sec. 25N do not apply. Sec. 25N applies to industrial establishments employing not less than one hundred workmen on an average per working day during the preceding twelve calendar months.

SECTION 25N: CONDITIONS PRECEDENT TO RETRENCHMENT OF WORKMEN

(1) No workman employed in any industrial establishment to which this Chapter applies, who has been in continuous service for not less than one year under an employer shall be retrenched by that employer until,–

(a) the workman has been given three months' notice in writing indicating the reasons for retrenchment

and the period of notice has expired, or the workman has been paid in lieu of such notice, wages for
the period of the notice; and

(b) the prior permission of the appropriate Government
or such authority as may be specified by that
Government by notification in the Official Gazette
(hereafter in this section referred to as the specified
authority) has been obtained on an application made
in this behalf.

(2) An application for permission under sub-section (1)
shall be made by the employer in the prescribed manner stating clearly the reasons for the intended retrenchment and a copy of such application shall also be served
simultaneously on the workman concerned in the prescribed manner.

(3) Where an application for permission under sub-section
(1) has been made, the appropriate Government or the
specified authority, after making such enquiry as it thinks
fit and after giving a reasonable opportunity of being
heard to the employer, the workmen concerned and
the persons interested in such retrenchment, may,
having regard to the genuineness and adequacy of the
reasons stated by the employer, the interests of the
workmen and all other relevant factors, by order and
for reasons to be recorded in writing, grant or refuse to
grant such permission and a copy of such order shall
be communicated to the employer and the workmen.

(4) Where an application for permission has been made
under sub-section (1) and the appropriate Government
or the specified authority does not communicate the
order granting or refusing to grant permission to the
employer within a period of sixty days from the date
on which such application is made, the permission applied for shall be deemed to have been granted on the
expiration of the said period of sixty days.

(5) An order of the appropriate Government or the specified authority granting or refusing to grant permission shall, subject to the provisions of sub-section (6), be final and binding on all the parties concerned and shall remain in force for one year from the date of such order.

(6) The appropriate Government or the specified authority may, either on its own motion or on the application made by the employer or any workman, review its order granting or refusing to grant permission under sub-section (3) or refer the matter or, as the case may be, cause it to be referred, to a Tribunal for adjudication:

Provided that where a reference has been made to a Tribunal under this sub-section, it shall pass an award within a period of thirty days from the date of such reference.

(7) Where no application for permission under sub-section (1) is made, or where the permission for any retrenchment has been refused, such retrenchment shall be deemed to be illegal from the date on which the notice of retrenchment was given to the workman and the workman shall be entitled to all the benefits under any law for the time being in force as if no notice had been given to him.

(8) Notwithstanding anything contained in the foregoing provisions of this section, the appropriate Government may, if it is satisfied that owing to such exceptional circumstances as accident in the establishment or death of the employer or the like, it is necessary so to do, by order, direct that the provisions of sub-section (1) shall not apply in relation to such establishment for such period as may be specified in the order.

(9) Where permission for retrenchment has been granted under sub-section (3) or where permission for retrenchment is deemed to be granted under sub-section (4), every workman who is employed in that establishment

immediately before the date of application for permission under this section shall be entitled to receive, at the time of retrenchment, compensation which shall be equivalent to fifteen days' average pay for every completed year of continuous service or any part thereof in excess of six months.

SECTION 25U: PENALTY FOR UNFAIR LABOUR PRACTICES

Any person who commits any unfair labour practice shall be punishable with imprisonment for a term which may extend to six months or with fine which may extend to one thousand rupees or with both.

SECTION 33: CONDITIONS OF SERVICE ETC. TO REMAIN UNCHANGED UNDER CERTAIN CIRCUMSTANCES DURING PENDENCY OF PROCEEDINGS

(1) During the pendency of any conciliation proceeding before a conciliation officer or a Board or any proceeding before an arbitrator or a Labour Court or Tribunal or National Tribunal in respect of an industrial dispute, no employer shall:

(a) in regard to any matter *connected* with the dispute, alter, to the prejudice of the workmen concerned in such dispute, the conditions of service applicable to them immediately before the commencement of such proceeding; or

(b) for any misconduct *connected* with the dispute, discharge or punish, whether by dismissal or otherwise, any workman concerned in such dispute, save with the *express permission in writing* of the authority before which the proceeding is pending.

(2) During the pendency of any such proceeding in respect of an industrial dispute, the employer may, in accordance with the standing orders applicable to a workman concerned in such dispute, or where there are no such standing orders, in accordance with the terms of the contract, whether express or implied, between him and the workman,-

(a) alter, in regard to any matter *not connected* with the dipute, the conditions of service applicable to that workman immediately before the commencement of such proceeding; or

(b) for any misconduct not connected with the dispute, discharge or punish, whether by dismissal or otherwise, that workman:

Provided that no such workman shall be discharged or dismissed, unless he has been paid wages for one month and an application has been made by the employer to the authority before which the proceeding is pending for approval of the action taken by the employer.

(3) Notwithstanding anything contained in sub-section (2), no employer shall during the pendency of any such proceeding in respect of an industrial dispute, take any action against any *protected workman* concerned in such dispute -

(a) by altering, to the prejudice of such *protected workman*, the conditions of service applicable to him immediately before the commencement of such proceedings; or

(b) by discharging or punishing, whether by dismissal or otherwise, such protected workman, save with the *express permission in writing* of the authority before which the proceeding is pending.

Explanation: For the purposes of this sub-section, a "protected workman", in relation to an establishment, means a workman who, being a member of the executive or other office-bearer of a registered trade union connected with the establishment, is recognised as such in accordance with rules made in this behalf.

(4) In every establishment, the number of workmen to be recognised as protected workmen for the purposes of sub-section (3) shall be one per cent of the total number of workmen employed therein subject to a minimum number of five protected workmen and a maximum number of one hundred protected workmen and for the distribution of such protected workmen among various trade unions, if any, connected with the establishment and the manner in which the workmen may be chosen and recognised as protected workmen.

(5) Where an employer makes an application to a conciliation officer, Board, an arbitrator, a Labour Court, Tribunal or National Tribunal under the proviso to sub-section (2) for approval of the action taken by him, the authority concerned shall, without delay, hear such application and pass, within a period of three months from the date of receipt of such application such order in relation thereto as it deems fit:

Provided that where any such authority considers it necessary or expedient to do so, it may, for reasons to be recorded in writing, extend such period by such further period as it may think fit:

Provided further that no proceedings before any such authority shall lapse merely on the ground that any period specified in this sub-section had expired without such proceedings being completed.

SECTION 36: REPRESENTATION OF THE PARTIES

(1) A workman who is a party to a dispute shall be entitled to be represented in any proceeding under this Act by:

(a) any member of the executive or other office-bearer of a registered trade union of which he is a member;

(b) any member of the executive or other office-bearer of a federation of trade unions to which the trade union referred to in clause (a) is affiliated;

(c) where the worker is not a member of any trade union, by any member of the executive or other office-bearer of any trade union connected with, or by any other workman employed in, the industry in which the worker is employed and authorized in such manner as may be prescribed.

(2) An employer who is a party to a dispute shall be entitled to be represented in any proceeding under this Act by:

(a) an officer of an association of employers of which he is a member,

(b) an officer of a federation of associations of employers to which the association referred to in clause (a) is affiliated;

(c) where the employer is not a member of any association of employers, by an officer of any association of employers connected with, or by any other employer engaged in, the industry in which the employer is engaged and authorized in such manner as may be prescribed.

(3) No party to a dispute shall be entitled to be represented by a legal practitioner in any conciliation proceedings under this Act or in any proceedings before a Court.

(4) In any proceeding before a Labour Court, Tribunal or National Tribunal, a party to a dispute may be represented by a legal practitioner with the consent of the other parties to the proceeding and with the leave of the Labour Court, Tribunal or National Tribunal, as the case may be.

THE SECOND SCHEDULE
(See Section 7)

MATTERS WITHIN THE JURISDICTION OF LABOUR COURTS

1. The propriety or legality of an order passed by an employer under the standing orders;
2. The application and interpretation of standing orders;
3. Discharge or dismissal or workmen including reinstatement of, or grant of relief to, workmen wrongfully dismissed;
4. Withdrawal of any customary concession or privilege;
5. Illegality or otherwise of a strike or lock-out; and
6. All matters other than those specified in the Third Schedule.

THE THIRD SCHEDULE
(See Section 7-A)

MATTERS WITHIN THE JURISDICTION OF INDUSTRIAL TRIBUNALS

1. Wages, including the period and mode of payment;
2. Compensatory and other allowances;
3. Hours of work and rest intervals;
4. Leave with wages and holidays;
5. Bonus, profit-sharing, provident fund and gratuity;
6. Shift-working otherwise than in accordance with standing orders;
7. Classification by grades;

8. Rules of discipline;
9. Rationalisation;
10. Retrenchment of workmen and closure of establishment; and
11. Any other matter that may be prescribed.

THE FIFTH SCHEDULE
[*See Section 2(ra)*]

UNFAIR LABOUR PRACTICES

I-On the Part of Employers and Trade Unions of Employers

1. To interfere with, restrain from, or coerce, workmen in the exercise of their right to organise, form, join or assist a trade union or to engage in concerted activities for the purposes of collective bargaining or other mutual aid or protection, that is to say:

    (a) threatening workmen with discharge or dismissal, if they join a trade union;
    (b) threatening a lock-out or closure, if a trade union is organised;
    (c) granting wage increase to workmen at crucial periods of trade union organisation, with a view to undermining the efforts of the trade union organisation.

2. To dominate, interfere with or contribute support, financial or otherwise, to any trade union, that is to say:

    (a) an employer taking an active interest in organising a trade union of his workmen; and
    (b) an employer showing partiality or granting favour to one of several trade unions attempting to organise

his workmen or to its members, where such a trade union is not a recognised trade union.

3. To establish employer-sponsored trade unions of workmen.

4. To encourage or discourage membership in any trade union by discriminating against any workman, that is to say:

   (a) discharging or punishing a workman, because he urged other workmen to join or organise a trade union;

   (b) discharging or dismissing a workman for taking part in any strike (not being a strike which it deemed to be an illegal strike under this Act);

   (c) changing seniority rating of workmen because of trade union activities;

   (d) refusing to promote workmen to higher posts on account of their trade union activities;

   (e) giving unmerited promotions to certain workmen with a view to creating discord amongst other workmen, or to undermine the strength of their trade union;

   (f) discharging office-bearers or active members of the trade union on account of their trade union activities.

5. To discharge or dismiss workmen:

   (a) by way of victimisation;

   (b) not in good faith, but in the colourable exercise of the employer's rights;

   (c) by falsely implicating a workman in a criminal case on false evidence or on concocted evidence;

   (d) for patently false reasons;

   (e) on untrue or trumped-up allegations of absence without leave;

   (f) in utter disregard of the principles of natural justice in the conduct of domestic enquiry or with undue haste;

    (g) for misconduct of a minor or technical character, without having any regard to the nature of the particular misconduct or the past record or service of the workmen, thereby leading to a disproportionate punishment.

6. To abolish the work of a regular nature being done by workmen, and to give such work to contractors as a measure of breaking a strike.

7. To transfer a workman *mala fide* from one place to another, under the guise of following management policy.

8. To insist upon individual workmen, who are on a legal strike, to sign a good conduct bond, as a precondition to allowing them to resume work.

9. To show favouritism or partiality to one set of workers regardless of merit.

10. To employ workmen as "badlis" casuals or temporaries and to continue them as such for years, with the object of depriving them of the status and privileges of permanent workmen.

11. To discharge or discriminate against any workman for filing charges or testifying against an employer in any enquiry or proceeding relating to any industrial dispute.

2. To recruit workmen during a strike which is not an illegal strike.

13. Failure to implement award, settlement or agreement.

14. To indulge in acts of force or violence.

15. To refuse to bargain collectively, in good faith with the recognised trade unions.

16. Proposing or continuing a lock-out deemed to be illegal under this Act.

II-On the part of Workmen and Trade Unions of Workmen

1. To advise or actively support or instigate any strike deemed to be illegal under this Act.

2. To coerce workmen in the exercise of their right to self-organisation or to join a trade union or refrain from joining any trade union, that is to say:

    (a) for a trade union or its members to picketing in such a manner that non-striking workmen are physically debarred from entering the work places;

    (b) to indulge in acts of force or violence or to hold out threats of intimidation in connection with a strike against non-striking workmen or against managerial staff.

3. For a recognised union to refuse to bargain collectively in good faith with the employer.

4. To indulge in coercive activities against certification of a bargaining representative.

5. To stage, encourage or instigate such forms of coercive actions as wilful "go slow", squatting on the work premises after working hours or "gherao" of any of the members of the managerial or other staff.

6. To stage demonstrations at the residences of the employers or the managerial staff members.

7. To incite or indulge in wilful damage to the employer's property connected with the industry.

8. To indulge in acts of force or violence or to hold out threats of intimidation against any workman with a view to prevent him from attending work.

****

Annexure 1B

The Industrial Employment (Standing Orders) Act, 1946
Relevant Excerpts

SECTION 10A: PAYMENT OF SUBSISTENCE ALLOWANCE

(1) Where any workman is suspended by the employer pending investigation or inquiry into complaints or charges of misconduct against him, the employer shall pay to such workman subsistence allowance:

    (a) at the rate of fifty per cent of the wages which the workman was entitled to immediately preceding the date of such suspension, for the first ninety days of the suspension; and

    (b) at the rate of seventy-five per cent of such wages for the remaining period of suspension if the delay in the completion of disciplinary proceedings against such workman is not directly attributable to the conduct of such workman.

(2) If any dispute arises regarding the subsistence allowance payable to a workman under sub-section (1), the workman or the employer concerned may refer the dispute to the Labour Court, constituted under the Industrial Disputes Act, 1947 (14 of 1947), within the local limits of whose jurisdiction the industrial establishment lies wherein such workman is employed is situated and the Labour Court to which the dispute is so referred shall, after giving the parties an opportunity of being heard, decide the dispute and such decision shall be final and binding on the parties.

(3) Notwithstanding anything contained in the foregoing provisions of this section, where provisions relating to payment of subsistence allowance under any other law for the time being in force in any State are more beneficial than the provisions of this section, the provisions of such other law shall be applicable to the payment of subsistence allowance in that State.

SECTION 12A: TEMPORARY APPLICATION OF MODEL STANDING ORDERS

(1) Notwithstanding anything contained in sections 3 to 12, for the period commencing on the date on which this Act becomes applicable to an industrial establishment and ending with the date on which the standing orders as finally certified under this Act come into operation under Section 7 in that establishment, the prescribed *model standing orders* shall be deemed to be adopted in that establishment, and the provisions of Section 9, sub-section (2) of Section 13 and Section 13–A shall apply to such model *standing orders* as they apply to the standing orders so certified.

(2) Nothing contained in sub-section (1) shall apply to an industrial establishment in respect of which the appropriate Government of the State of Maharashtra.

THE SCHEDULE
[See Sections 2(g) and 3 (2)]

MATTERS TO BE PROVIDED IN STANDING ORDERS UNDER THIS ACT

1. Classification of workmen, e.g. whether permanent, temporary, apprentices, probationers, or *badlis*.

2. Manner of intimating to workmen periods and hours of work, holidays, pay-days and wage-rates.

3. Shift working.

4. Attendance and late coming.

5. Conditions of, procedure in applying for, and the authority which may grant, leave and holidays.

6. Requirement to enter premises by certain gates, and liability to search.

7. Closing and reopening of sections of the industrial establishment, and temporary stoppages of work and the rights and liabilities of the employer and workmen arising therefrom.

8. Termination of employment, and the notice thereof to be given by employer and workmen.

9. Suspension or dismissal for misconduct and acts or omissions which constitute misconduct.

10. Means of redress for workmen against unfair treatment or wrongful exactions by the employer or his agents or servants.

10A. Additional matters to be provided in standing orders relating to industrial establishments in coal mines:

(1) Medical aid in case of accident.

(2) Railways travel facilities.

(3) Method of filling vacancies.

(4) Transfers.

(5) Liability of manager of the establishments of mine.

(6) Service certificate.

(7) Exhibition and supply of standing orders.

11. Any other matter which may be prescribed.

****

Annexure 1C

The Industrial Employment (S.O.) Central Rules, 1946–Model Standing Orders
Relevant Excerpts

SCHEDULE-I

MODEL STANDING ORDERS IN RESPECT OF
INDUSTRIAL ESTABLISHMENT NOT BEING
INDUSTRIAL ESTABLISHMENTS IN COAL MINES

1. Termination of Employment: Paragraph 13

(1) For terminating the employment of a permanent workman, notice in writing shall be given either by the employer or the workman—one month's notice in the case of monthly rated workmen, and two weeks' notice in the case of other workmen; one month's or two weeks' pay, as the case may be, may be paid in lieu of notice.

(2) No temporary workmen, whether monthly-rated, weekly-rated or piece-rated and no probationer or *badli* shall be entitled to any notice or pay in lieu thereof if his services are terminated as a punishment unless he has been given an opportunity of explaining the charges of misconduct alleged against him in the manner prescribed in paragraph 14.

(3) Where the employment of any workman is terminated, the wages earned by him and other dues, if any, shall be paid before the expiry of the second working day from the day on which his employment is terminated.

2. Disciplinary Action for Misconduct: Paragraph 14

(1) A workman may be fined up to two per cent of his wages in a month for any of the following acts and omissions, namely:

Note-Specify the acts and omissions which the employer may notify with the previous approval of the ... Government or of the prescribed authority in pursuance of Section 8 of the Payment of Wages Act, 1936.

(2) A workman may be suspended for a period not exceeding four days at a time, or dismissed without notice or any compensation in lieu of notice if he is found to be guilty of misconduct.

(3) The following acts and omissions shall be treated as misconduct:

    (a) wilful insubordination or disobedience, whether alone or in combination with others to any lawful and reasonable order of a superior;

    (b) theft, fraud or dishonesty in connection with the employer's business or property;

    (c) wilful damage to or loss of employer's goods or property;

    (d) taking or giving bribes or any illegal gratification;

    (e) habitual late attendance;

    (f) habitual breach of any law applicable to the establishment;

    (g) riotous or disorderly behaviour during working hours at the establishment or any act subversive of discipline;

    (h) habitual negligence or neglect of work;

    (i) frequent repetition of any act or omission for which a fine may be imposed to a maximum of 2 per cent of the wages in a month; and

(j)   striking work or inciting others to strike work in contravention of the provisions of any law, or rule having the force of law.

(4)(a) where a disciplinary proceeding against a workman is contemplated or is pending or where criminal proceedings against him in respect of any offence are under investigation or trial and the employer is satisfied that it is necessary or desirable to place the workman under suspension, he may, by order in writing, suspend him with effect from such date as may be specified in the order. A Statement setting out in detail the reasons for such suspension shall be supplied to the workman within a week from the date of suspension.

(b)   A workman who is placed under suspension shall be paid a subsistence allowance in accordance with the provisions of Section 10–A of the Act.

(ba) In the enquiry, the workman shall be entitled to appear in person or to be represented by an office-bearer of a trade union of which he is a member.

(bb) The proceedings of the enquiry shall be recorded in Hindi or in English, or the language of the State where the industrial establishment is located, whichever is preferred by the workman.

(bc) The proceedings of the enquiry shall be completed within a period of three months:

Provided that the period of three months may, for reasons to be recorded in writing, be extended by such further period as may be deemed necessary by the enquiry officer.

(c)   If on the conclusion of the enquiry or, as the case may be, of the criminal proceedings, the workman has been found guilty of the charges framed against him and it is considered after giving the workman concerned reasonable opportunity of making representation on the penalty proposed, that an order of dismissal or suspension or fine or stoppage of annual increment or reduction in rank would meet the ends of justice, the employer shall pass an order accordingly:

Provided that when an order of dismissal is passed under this clause, the workman shall be deemed to have been absent from duty during the period of suspension and shall not be entitled to any remuneration for such period, and the subsistence allowance already paid to him shall not be recovered:

Provided further that where the period between the date on which the workman was suspended from duty pending the enquiry or investigation or trial and the date on which an order of suspension was passed under this clause exceeds four days, the workman shall be deemed to have been suspended only for four days or for such shorter period as is specified in the said order of suspension and for the remaining period he shall be entitled to the same wages as he would have received if he had not been placed under suspension, after deducting the subsistence allowance paid to him for such period:

Provided also that where an order imposing fine or stoppage of annual increment or reduction in rank is passed under this clause, the workman shall be deemed to have been on duty during the period of suspension and shall be entitled to the same wages as he would have received if he had not been placed under suspension after deducting the subsistence allowance paid to him for such period:

Provided also that in the case of a workman to whom the provisions of clause (2) of Article 311 of the Constitution apply, the provisions of that Article shall be complied with.

(d) If on the conclusion of the inquiry, or as the case may be, of the criminal proceedings, the workman has been found to be not guilty of any of the charges framed against him, he shall be deemed to have been on duty during the period of suspension and shall be entitled to the same wages as he would have received if he had not been placed under paid to him for such period.

(e) The payment of subsistence allowance under this standing order, shall be subject to the workman concerned not taking up any employment during the period of suspension.

(5) In awarding punishment under this standing order, the authority imposing the punishment shall take into account the gravity of misconduct the previous record, if any, of the workman and any other extenuating or aggravating circumstances, that may exist. A copy of the order passed by the authority imposing the punishment shall be supplied to the workman concerned.

(5) (a) A workman aggrieved by an order imposing punishment may, within twenty-one days from the date of receipt of the order, appeal to the appellate authority;

(b) the employer shall, for the purposes of clause (a) specify the appellate authority;

(c) the appellate authority, after giving an opportunity to the workman of being heard, shall pass such order as he thinks proper on the appeal within fifteen days of its receipt and communicate the same to the workman in writing.

****

Industrial Employment (S.O.) Central Rules, 1946–Model Standing Orders Applicable to Coal Mines
(Relevant Portions)

SCHEDULE 1A

1. Loss of Lien on Appointment: Standing Order No. 10(e)

If a workman remains absent beyond the period of leave originally granted or subsequently extended, he shall lose lien on his appointment unless he:

(a) returns within ten days of expiry of his leave, and

(b) explains to the satisfaction of the manager his inability to return on the expiry of his leave.

In case the workman loses, as aforesaid, his lien on the appointment, he shall be entitled to be kept on the 'badli list'.

2. Termination of Services: Standing Order No. 13

(a) For terminating the services of a permanent workman having less than one year of continuous service, notice of one month in writing with reasons or wages in lieu thereof shall be given by the employer:

Provided that no such notice shall be required to be given when the services of the workman are terminated on account of misconduct established in accordance with the standing orders.

(b) Subject to the provisions of the Industrial Disputes Act, 1947, no notice of termination of employment shall be necessary in the case of temporary and "badli" workman:

Provided that a temporary workman 'who has completed three months' continuous service shall be given two weeks' notice of the intention to terminate his employment, if such termination is not in accordance with the terms of the contract of his employment:

Provided further that when the services of a temporary workman, who has not completed three months' continuous service, are terminated before the completion of the term of employment given to him, he shall be informed of the reasons in writing. When the services of a "badli" workman are terminated before the return to work of the permanent incumbent or the expiry of his (badli's) term of employment, he shall be informed of the reasons for such termination in writing.

(c) No workman shall leave the service of an employer unless notice in writing is given at the scale indicated below:

(i) for monthly paid workmen   One month
(ii) for weekly paid workmen   Two weeks:

Provided that it will be for the employer to relax this condition and the workman may pay cash in lieu of such notice.

(d) For purposes of standing orders 13(a).(b), and (c), the terms 'service' and 'wages' shall have the same meaning as assigned to these in Section 25(B) (1) and 2 (rr) respectively of the Industrial Disputes Act, 1947.

3. DISCIPLINARY ACTION FOR MISCONDUCT: STANDING ORDER NO. 17

(i) A workman may be suspended by the employer pending investigation or departmental enquiry and shall be paid subsistence allowance in accordance with the provisions of Section 10–A of the Act. The payment of subsistence allowance shall be subject to the workman not taking any employment elsewhere during the period of suspension.

The following shall denote misconduct:

(a) Theft, fraud, or dishonesty in connection with the employer's business or property.

(b) Taking or giving of bribes or an illegal gratification whatsoever in connection with the employer's business or property.

(c) Wilful insubordination or disobedience, whether alone or in conjunction with another or others, or of any lawful or reasonable order of a superior. The order of the superior should normally be in writing.

(d) Habitual late attendance and habitual absence without leave or without sufficient cause.

(e) Drunkenness, fighting or riotous, disorderly or indecent behaviour while on duty or the place of work.

(f) Habitual neglect of work.

(g) Habitual indiscipline.

(h) Smoking underground or within the mine area in places where it is prohibited.

(i) Causing wilful damage to work in progress or to property of the employer.

(j) Sleeping on duty.

(k) Malingering or slowing down work.

(l) Acceptance of gifts from subordinate employees.

(m) Conviction in any Court of Law for any criminal offence involving *moral turpitude*.

(n) Continuous absence without permission and without satisfactory cause for more than ten days.

(o) Giving false information regarding one's name, age, father's name, qualification or previous service at the time of the employment.

(p) Leave work without permission or sufficient reason.

(q) Any breach of the Mines Act, 1952, or any other Act or any rules, regulations or by-laws thereunder, or of any Standing Orders.

(r) Threatening, abusing or assaulting any superior or co-worker.

(s) Habitual money-lending.

(t) Preaching of or inciting to violence.

(u) Abetment of or attempt at abetment or any of the above acts or misconduct.

(v) Going on illegal strike either singly or with other workers without giving 14 days' previous notice.

(w) Disclosing to any unauthorised person of any confidential information in regard to the working or process of the establishment which may come into the possession of the workman in the course of his work.

(x) Refusal to accept any chargesheet or order or notice communicated in writing.

(y) Failure or refusal to wear or use any protective equipment given by the employers.

(ii) No order of punishment under Standing Order No. 17(i) shall be made unless the workman concerned is informed in writing of the alleged misconduct and is given an opportunity to explain the allegations made against him. A departmental enquiry shall be instituted before dealing with the charges. During the period of enquiry, the workman concerned may be suspended. The workman may take the assistance of a co-worker to help him in the enquiry, if he so desires; the records of the departmental enquiry shall be kept in writing. The approval of the owner, agent or the chief mining engineer of the employer or a person holding similar position shall be obtained before imposing the punishment of dismissal. At the end of the enquiry, proceedings shall be given to the workman concerned on the conclusion of the enquiry on request by the workman.

(iii) If a workman is not found guilty of the charge framed against him, he shall be deemed to be on duty during the full period of his suspension and he shall be entitled to receive the same wages as he would have received if he had not been suspended.

(iv) In awarding punishment under the Standing Order, the authority awarding punishment shall take into account the gravity of misconduct, the previous record, if any, of the workman and any other extenuating or aggravating circumstances that may exist. A copy of the order passed by the authority awarding punishment shall be supplied to the workman concerned.

Annexure 2A

Case Studies for Exercises in Drafting Chargesheets

RAINBOW ENGINEERING WORKS

Rana Pratap, a helper in the mechanical maintenance department, applied for ten days' leave on August 19, 1999, to go to his native place. His leave was regretted by his foreman as the other helper Babulal was also on sick leave.

From August 19, 1999, Rana Pratap absented himself from duty. On August 22, 1999, he sent an application to the foreman seeking leave on medical grounds. This was accompanied by a medical certificate from the civil assistant surgeon certifying that Rana Pratap was suffering from high fever. He was recommended medical leave for 15 days from August 19, 1999.

While unauthorized absence from duty is a misconduct as per the company's Standing Order No. 23(ix), a permanent employee is entitled to 30 days' medical leave on half pay every calendar year if his sickness is certified by a registered medical practitioner. As on August 19, 1999, Rana Pratap had 25 days' medical leave to his credit.

How would you handle this case?

****

Annexure 2B

Lakshmi Manufacturing Company

Lakshmi Manufacturing Company is a registered factory employing 550 people. It produces spare parts for cars and scooters. Its security staff at the gate are vigilant and regularly check people/vehicles going out of the factory to prevent theft of the company's material.

On June 18, 1999, at 11 am, Rakesh, a material chaser in the services department went to the stores department to draw ten new GEC electric switches (15 amperes each) for some urgent breakdown job. Thereafter, he came to the cooperative credit society office to enquire about his loan application. At 11.30 am he suddenly remembered that he had to purchase a post-card from the post office (situated just outside the works gate), to write an urgent letter and thereafter go to his department, situated at a distance of about 1 km from the stores department. The distance between the stores department and the works gate is about 50 metres. Rakesh works in the general shift, i.e., from 7 am to 11.30 am and 12.30 pm to 4 pm. The lunch break is from 11.30 am to 12.30 pm. During this period, workers are allowed to go out of the premises.

At 11.35 am, there was a telephone call to S. M. Kumar, manager, services department from the security inspector, Ramanand, that one Rakesh, T. No. 321 had been caught red-handed at the gate by two sepoys, Ramadhin and Trilochan, while trying to go out of the factory premises with ten new GEC electric switches that were in a bag on his cycle.

In the preliminary enquiry, Rakesh confessed in writing that he was carrying the switches by mistake as he intended to come back to his department after buying a post-card. As per the procedure for drawing materials in the services department on the basis of a written instruction in the log book from the foreman, the material chaser has to prepare the material requisition after entering the details himself in the material requisition register. After getting the requisition signed by the foreman and the departmental head, he has to go to the stores department to draw the material. If the material is heavy, he has to arrange for transport. Rakesh carried small items like switches, fuses, etc., himself, to the department. Thereafter, he is supposed to hand over the material to the foreman and obtain his signature in the materials requistion register.

The log book as well as the materials requisition register showed that Rakesh had correctly entered the GEC electric switches therein.

As per the Standing Order No. 17(iii) of the company's certified standing orders, "Theft, fraud or dishonesty in connection with Company's business or property", is a misconduct warranting dismissal as per Standing Order No. 18. The manager can issue a chargesheet and also punish with dismissal any employee of his department who is alleged to have committed an act of misconduct.

Advise the manager, services department, on the steps required to be taken in this case. Assuming that a chargesheet is to be issued, please draft one.

****

Annexure 2C

PIONEER ENGINEERING WORKS

On every working day, when the works canteen of the Pioneer Engineering Works Company opens at 8 am, there is a big rush of employees for the purchase of tea and snacks. The canteen remains open for 30 minutes and all employees usually stand in the queue to make their purchases.

On February 14, 1999, at about 8.15 am, Joginder, *khalasy*, bearing token no. 45, who normally avoids standing in the queue, tried to purchase the snacks through Vipin, a co-worker, bearing token No. 108, who was in the queue. Ramlal, another worker, bearing token No. 111, who was standing just behind Vipin objected to this. An argument began between Joginder and Ramlal and in the process, Joginder slapped Ramlal. The canteen supervisor Babulal intervened and separated them.

As per the company's certified Standing Order No. 23(i), 'Riotous, disorderly or indecent behaviour within the company's premises', is a misconduct. The works manager is the disciplinary authority as per the Standing Orders. Advise the works manager on the steps for handling this case.

****

Annexure 2D

DIPIKA ENTERPRISES

In addition to large industrial complexes, a number of satellite industrial areas have mushroomed with a number of medium and small-scale ancillary units manufacturing a variety of products. Dipika Enterprises is a factory, which manufactures paints which are used by other industries. It has about 150 employees including three officers and 12 supervisory staff. The factory runs in two shifts. The morning shift starts from 6 am to 2 pm and the afternoon shift from 2 pm to 10 pm. The company does not provide any housing accommodation to the bulk of its workers who come from the neighbouring villages.

On May 12, 1999, Ramu, a mechanical fitter, was scheduled to work in the morning shift. However, his son who was sick needed to see a doctor. His house is situated at a distance of about 4 kms from the factory. At about 5 am, he came to the house of Kali Prasad, a warehouse *khalasy* who lives in the same village and gave him an application addressed to his foreman for one day's casual leave. He requested Kali Prasad to personally explain to the foreman the reason for the application. Kali Prasad went to the foreman's office at 8.30 am during the tea-break and learnt that because of a serious breakdown in the pump-room, all the mechanical staff including Narayan, the foreman, were busy. Kali Prasad left Ramu's application on the foreman's table and came back to work. The breakdown was set right after 2 pm. When the foreman came to his office at 3 pm, he found Ramus' leave application. He rejected his request and marked him absent for the day.

On May 13, 1999, during the tea-break after 8 am, the foreman reprimanded Ramu in his cabin. There was some altercation between the two, and attracted by the loud voices, others around also went inside the foreman's cabin. Apart from the assistant foreman Wadia, Prakash (time-keeper), Anil (helper), Motichand and Krishna (*mazdoors*), also came there. All of them heard Ramu threaten the foreman that if his leave for May 12, 1999, was not sanctioned, the foreman would face the consequences.

As per the company's Standing Order No. 23(i) "absenting without information/permission" is a misconduct. Also, as per the Standing Order No. 23(iv), "threatening or intimidating any employee within the boundaries of the works or company's premises" is a misconduct. The works manager is the competent authority to take disciplinary action. Help him to handle this case.

****

Annexure 2E

SHABNAM INDUSTRIES

On February 28, 1999, at about 6.45 pm, the duty officer (security), M. Kumar at the works gate, informed S. Rathod, an electrical engineer, that Narayan, a foreman of his department had been caught red-handed at the works gate while attempting to steal a small electric motor and certain other spare parts used in the electrical department. Rathod was requested to come to the security control room, where a preliminary enquiry was to be held.

During the preliminary enquiry, it was discovered that Narayan, personal no. 5824, foreman, came to the works gate at 6:15 pm on his Suvega autocycle bearing registration No. BRX 1421 (the number was not clearly visible). The works guard on duty Krishna Bahadur asked Narayan to stop and open the tool-box in which only an empty tiffin-box was found. Since the drivers' seat appeared to be thicker and of unusual size, the works guard questioned Narayan about it. Not being satisfied with the reply, he gave it a jerk and found that Narayan had constructed a box under the seat where a 0.50 horse power motor and eight 5 amperes switches belonging to the company were concealed. On being asked, Narayan replied that he had attended a breakdown after 5 pm. in the mill and replaced one 0.50 horse power motor. The motor that was recovered was the defective one. He could not return it as the store-issuer had already left for home after his duty which ended at 5 pm. He thought he would return the motor next day, as he had done many times in the past. He, however, could not explain why he was carrying the 5 amperes switches. Nor did not he give any satisfactory reason for not keeping the materials in the exterior, visible tool-box. On checking up at the security control room, in the presence of Narayan, it was found that the electric motor recovered was in working condition.

As per the company's certified Standing Order No. 23(iii), "theft. fraud, or dishonesty in connection with the company's business or property" is a misconduct. Advise the works manager on the steps for handling the above case.

****

Annexure 2F

CALCUTTA STEELS LTD

In some companies where the employees' children are given preference in employment, second or third generation workers develop a greater sense of commitment and loyalty to the organization. Even when grievances occur well-established, mutually acceptable systems and procedures ensure that such matters are settled through negotiation. One such company is Calcutta Steels Ltd., which employs 300 persons including over 250 in the worker's category. This company traditionally gives permanent employment subject to suitability, to one relative—the son, daughter, or son-in-law—of an employee, who retires after twenty years' service. An employee can get the name of his relation registered for employment after completing fifteen years' service. The management however is very rigid about verification of the relationship of the 'nominee' for employment.

Taking advantage of large-scale unemployment, some employees in the past tried to register persons other than relatives for employment, in return for pecuniary benefits. A few cases of such fraudulent attempts were detected, and as a consequence, these employees were warned and debarred from this facility.

On May 25, 1999, Chandu, T. No. 205, a chargeman, applied to the personnel officer to register the name of his son Bimal, aged 19 years, for employment in the company. On June 1, 1999, the personnel officer called him along with his son to complete the registration formalities. A verification of Bimals' school certificate, revealed that his real name was Bimal Kumar Mishra, son of Radhakant Mishra. On checking up Chandus' personal file it was found that on October 14, 1968, he was registered for employment on the application of Radhika, Ex. T. No. 035, who claimed Chandu to be her son-in-law, married to her daughter, Kulwati. Chandu also gave a statement to this effect.

As per the company's certified Standing Order No. 17(v) "Giving of false information of any kind either at the time of employment or thereafter, for securing any privilege from company", is a misconduct. Advise the works manager on the steps required in this case.

****

Annexure 2G

KRISHNA TRADING

M/s. Krishna Trading is a road transport company in Calcutta that owns a fleet of trucks that carry steel scrap-cuttings from various industrial organizations in Jamshedpur to a number of iron and steel foundries around Calcutta. Since the scrap is to be collected from various points at regular intervals, the company sends each truck with one driver and a cleaner-cum-*khalasy*. Its resident representative at Jamshedpur coordinates this effort from various locations. Scrap is generally loaded in the truck with the help of an overhead crane belonging to the company selling the scrap. During the time the empty truck is weighed, the material is loaded, as well as when the loaded truck is weighed, a representative each of the security department, accounts department (weight bridge) and of the department to which the scrap belonged, are present and a record of weights kept in a register. Since the contractor is keen to load the material quickly on the truck, his representative has to keep good relations with the crane drivers and the security staff. Things were running smoothly till Kali Charan, a representative of M/s. Krishna Trading, informed N. Raman, manager of the factory, that on the morning of April 1, 1999 the crane driver Ramu, had threatened to damage the truck by dropping the scrap from a height unless he was given Rs. 20/- per truck load. The security *havaldar* K. P. Singh also demanded Rs. 50/- per truck load to expedite the loading and weighing. Kali Charan also complained that on earlier occasions, he used to pay Rs. 5/- to the crane driver and Rs. 20/- to the security *havaldar* per truck to avoid delay in loading and weighment.

Raman was concerned over the dishonest behaviour of his employees and called the security officer, Captain Ranjit Singh. Raman put his initials on seven ten–rupee new currency notes and gave them to Kali Charan to hand over to the *havaldar*, K. P. Singh and the Ramu on demand for their so-called services. He also advised Captain Ranjit Singh to lay a trap to catch these employees.

On completion of the loading at about 11 am on April 1, 1999, Ramu was given two of the ten–rupee notes, and after the weighing, *havaldar* K. P. Singh was given five ten–rupee notes.

After the loaded truck was escorted outside the works at about 11.05 am, Captain Singh called *havaldar* K. P. Singh and Ramu to the security office where apart from Raman and Kali Charan, the administrative officer, Goel, was also present. In their presence, Captain Singh asked *havaldar* K. P. Singh and Ramu to take out whatever money they had with them. In the process, all the signed currency notes were recovered. At the instance of Raman, Goel took down the statements of Kali Charan, K. P. Singh, Ramu and Captain Ranjit Singh.

Both *havaldar* K. P. Singh and Ramu admitted their mistake and offered an apology, but refused to put their signatures on the written statement. There was a *prima facie* case against both *havaldar* K. P. Singh and Ramu.

As per the company's Standing Order No. 23(iii) "taking or giving bribe or illegal gratification whatsoever", is a misconduct. How would you handle this case?

Annexure 3

DRAFTING A CHARGESHEET

A chargesheet is the primary document on which the entire proceedings of enquiry will be based. The employee in order to defend himself, must know precisely the nature of the allegations made against him. This is necessary as per the rule, *audi alteram partem*. Since the object of a chargesheet is to ascertain what the employee has to say in his defence against the allegations, it should be drafted in simple language avoiding any scope for ambiguity. If it relates to an incident, the date, place and time should be clearly mentioned. Before drafting a chargesheet, it is desirable to obtain a written report/complaint, and in appropriate cases, conduct a preliminary enquiry to ascertain the exact nature of the allegation.

Sometimes, in the anxiety to issue a chargesheet promptly due to pressure from superiors, or for other reasons, the drafting is vague and ambiguous. A chargesheet should be drafted only when all the relevant facts are made available and with proper application of mind. Although the law on the subject is more or less clear, people issue defective chargesheets.

While the perception of individuals will continue to differ, it is necessary to understand what constitutes a defective chargesheet as against the requirements of a valid chargesheet. An example here would help to elucidate the point in issue. Let us look at the facts in the case of Lakshmi Manufacturing Company in Annexure 2B. Given below are two draft chargesheets. After going through their contents, decide for yourself which one has been properly framed.

DRAFT CHARGESHEET 1

Ref. No. CS/6/99
June 18, 1999

Mr. Rakesh – T. No. 321
Material Chaser, Services Department

Today you were caught red-handed by the security sepoys at the works gate while trying to go out of the works with the company's property during the lunch-break. During the preliminary enquiry held for the purpose after the incident, you accepted that you were carrying the above material by mistake and you intended to come back to the works after purchasing a post-card for writing an urgent letter. This plea is not acceptable to the management.

Any attempt at theft of the company's property is a misconduct as per our Standing Order warranting dismissal.

You are directed to show cause why necessary action to dismiss you may not be taken.

(S. M. Kumar)
Manager, Services Department

DRAFT CHARGESHEET 2

Ref. No. CS/6/99
June 18, 1999

Mr. Rakesh – T. No. 321
Material Chaser,
Services Department

It has been reported that on June 18, 1999, at about 11.35 am while you were trying to go out of the works, security sepoys Ramadhin and Trilochan, who were on duty at the works gate, recovered 10 new GEC electric switches (15 amperes each) belonging to the company, from the bag hanging from your cycle handle.

The above act on your part constitutes misconduct as per Standing Order No. 17(iii) of the company's certified Standing Orders.

Please explain in writing within 48 hours of the receipt of this chargesheet as to why disciplinary action should not be taken against you for the above misconduct.

(S. M. Kumar)
Manager, Services Dept

In Draft No. 2, the charge is more specific. There is no irrelevant information/remarks which does not constitute a charge requiring an explanation.

Annexure 4

Ref. No. ENQ/6/99
June 24, 1999

DRAFTING AN OFFICE ORDER

Mr. Rakesh, T. No. 321, material chaser, services department, was issued a chargesheet No. CS/6/99 of June 18, 1999, to which he has submitted an explanation on June 20, 1999, denying the charges. As the explanation submitted by Mr. Rakesh is unsatisfactory, it has been decided to hold an enquiry. Mr. P. Basu, personnel manager, is hereby appointed Enquiry Officer to conduct an enquiry of the aforesaid chargesheet as per procedure. Mr. Ramanand, inspector, security department, is hereby nominated as management representative to conduct the managements' case in the enquiry.

(S. M. Kumar)
Manager, Services Department

c.c.   Mr. P. Basu, personnel manager, for information. He is requested to conduct the enquiry as per procedure and submit his findings early.

cc.   Mr. Ramanand, inspector, security department with all connected papers for information and needful action.

cc.   Mr. Rakesh, T. No. 321, material chaser, for information.

Annexure 5

Ref. No. PM/ENQ/6/99
June 26, 1999

DRAFTING A NOTICE OF ENQUIRY

Mr. Rakesh – T. No. 321
Material Chaser,
Services Department

Through Proper Channel

Please refer to your copy of the Office Order No. ENQ/6/99 of June 24, 1999 issued by the manager, services department, appointing me as enquiry officer in connection with the chargesheet No. CS/6/99 of June 18, 1999 issued to you.

I shall hold the enquiry of the above chargesheet in my office in the administrative building on June 30, 1999 at 10 am. During the enquiry, you will be given reasonable opportunity to defend yourself by cross-examining the management's witnesses/documents and examining your own witnesses/documents.

You are directed to attend the aforesaid enquiry with your witnesses, etc., if any. Please note, if you fail to attend the enquiry without showing sufficient reasons in advance, the same will be held ex parte.

(P. Basu)
Enquiry Officer and Personnel Manager

c.c. Mr. Ramanand, inspector, security department and management representative for information.

Annexure 6

ORDER SHEET

PROCEEDINGS OF THE DOMESTIC ENQUIRY RELATING TO CHARGESHEET NO.CS/6/99 DATED JUNE 18, 1999, ISSUED TO MR. RAKESH, MATERIAL CHASER, T. NO. 321, SERVICES DEPARTMENT

Date and Time

25.6.99   Received from Mr S. M. Kumar, Manager Services Dept. Ref. ENQ/6/99 dated June 24, 1989. appointing me as enquiry officer to conduct an enquiry in respect of the above chargesheet. Mr. Ramanand, inspector, security, has been nominated as the management representative.

Sd/ P. Basu
25.6.99

26.6.99   Notice issued to Mr. Rakesh vide Ref. No. PM/ENQ/6/99 dated June 26, 1999, informing him that the enquiry will be held on June 30, 1999 at 10 am in the office of the undersigned. Carbon copy of the notice was sent to the management representative for information.

Sd/ P. Basu
26.6.99

30.6.99   The management representative Mr. Ramanand was present. The chargesheeted employee Mr. Rakesh was also present with his union representative, Mr. Rajendra. The contents of the chargesheet were read out and explained to the chargesheeted employee. He did not accept the charge. The procedure to be followed during the enquiry was explained to both the parties. The management representative produced the following exhibits:

1. Ten new GEC electric switches recovered from Mr. Rakesh on June 18, 1999 marked MEX–1

2. Statement of Mr. Rakesh recorded on June 18, 1999 marked MEX–2 (in two pages)

3. Statements of Mr. Trilochan and Mr. Ramadhin recorded on June 18, 1999 marked MEX–3 (in two pages)

sd/ P. Basu 30.6.99
sd/ Ramanand
sd/ Rakesh
sd/ Rajendra

The following management witnesses were examined one by one and cross-examined by the chargesheeted employee:

1. Mr. Trilochan,
   security sepoy   ...... MWI
2. Mr. Ramadhin,
   security sepoy   ...... MW2 sd/ all concerned

The enquiry was adjourned at 1 pm for lunch. Parties to reassemble at 2:30 pm

sd/ P. Basu 30.6.99
sd/ Ramanand
sd/ Rakesh
sd/ Rajendra

2.30 pm   All concerned are present. The chargesheeted employee produced Mr. S. Narayan, general foreman, as his only defence witness and the following exhibits

1. Log Book for 1999 marked as   ......: WEX–1
2. Material Requisition Register for
    1999 marked as WEX–2

                                sd/ P. Basu 30.6.99
                                sd/ Ramanand
                                sd/ Rakesh
                                sd/ Rajendra

Mr. Narayan, WWI, was examined by Mr. Rakesh and cross-examined by Mr. Ramanand. In the end, the chargesheeted employee gave his statement. He was cross-examined by the management representative. Thereafter, the enquiry was closed at 5 pm.

                                sd/ P. Basu 30.6.99
                                sd/ Ramanand
                                sd/ Rakesh
                                sd/ Rajendra

2.7.99   Enquiry report submitted to Mr. S. M. Kumar, manager, services department, together with all the statements/exhibits.

                                sd/ P. Basu 2.7.99

Annexure 7

FORMAT OF AN ENQUIRY REPORT

An enquiry report in respect of chargesheet No. CS/6/99, dated June 18, 1999 issued to Mr. Rakesh. T. No., material chaser, services department.

1. Case in brief:
2. Chargesheet and reply:
   (preferably quote; in appropriate cases, paraphrase)
3. Appointment of Enquiry Officer: (give reference)
4. The Enquiry:

   - Date(s) of enquiry:
   - Witnesses examined/exhibits produced from both sides:
   - Issues for consideration:
   - Analysis of the statements (with reasoning for accepting or discarding any evidence, look for corroboration or circumstantial evidence)
   - Findings and conclusion.

Annexure 8

LETTER TO A DELINQUENT EMPLOYEE
AFTER FINALIZATION OF THE ENQUIRY

Ref. PUN/PP/6/99
July 3, 1999

Mr. Rakesh, T. No. 321
Material Chaser,
Services Department

Please refer to the chargesheet No. CS/6/99 of June 18, 1999 issued to you for attempted theft of 10 new GEC electric switches (15 amperes each) on June 18, 1999 belonging to the company, which was detected by security sepoys Ramadhin and Trilochan at the works gate at about 11.35 am while you were trying to go out of the works.

As your explanation to the above chargesheet was found unsatisfactory, an enquiry was conducted by Mr. P. Basu, the personnel manager, who was appointed enquiry officer as per office order No. ENQ/6/99 of June 24, 1989.

On completion of the enquiry, the enquiry officer has submitted to me his findings together with the enquiry proceedings and the exhibits. As per the evidence adduced during the enquiry, the enquiry officer has found you guilty of the charge of attempted theft of 10 new GEC electric switches (15 amperes each) belonging to the company on June 18, 1999. I have gone through the enquiry proceedings.

However, before I finally decide about your guilt or otherwise and impose punishment, I am enclosing a copy of the report of the enquiry officer holding you guilty of the charges levelled, for your views if any. Your views/comments should reach the undersigned within three days of receipt of this letter for further consideration if required.

Please note that if I do not hear from you within the stipulated period, I shall presume that you have no comments to make on the findings of the enquiry officer and action as per the company's standing orders will follow accordingly.

(S. M. Kumar)
Manager, Services Department

Annexure 9

LETTER OF DISMISSAL

Ref. PUN/6/99
July 7, 1999

Mr. Rakesh, T. No. 321
Material Chaser,
Services Department

Please refer to the chargesheet No. CS/6/99 of June 18, 1999, issued to you for attempted theft of 10 new GEC electric switches (15 amperes each), on June 18, 1999, belonging to the company, which was detected by security sepoys Ramadhin and Trilochan at the works gate at about 11.35 am while you were trying to go out of the works.

As your explanation to the above chargesheet was found unsatisfactory, an enquiry was conducted by Mr. P. Basu, personnel manager, who was appointed enquiry officer as per office order No. ENQ/6/99 of June 24, 1999.

On completion of the enquiry, the enquiry officer submitted to me his findings together with the enquiry proceedings and the exhibits. As per the evidence adduced during the enquiry, the enquiry officer found you guilty of the charge levelled.

In this connection, I had forwarded to you a copy of the enquiry report vide letter No. PUN/PP/6/99 of July 3, 1999 for your views/comments if any. I have gone though the points raised by you in this connection on the findings of the enquiry officer. Since you have raised no fresh points, and as you have been found guilty of a serious act of misconduct as per Standing Order No.17(iii) of the company's certified standing orders, you are hereby dismissed from the service of the company.

You may collect your dues from the accounts department after handing over the company's property and quarters if any, in your possession.

(S. M. Kumar)
Manager, Services Department

c.c. Accounts Department

List of Case Laws

MISCONDUCT

1. *Agnani (WM) vs Badridas and Others 1963 I LLJ 684 SC*
2. *Tata Oil Mills Co. Ltd. vs Their Workmen 1964 II LLJ 113 SC*
3. *Glaxo Laboratories(I) Ltd. vs Labour Court Meerut & Others 1984 I LLJ 16 SC*
4. *Rashiklal V. Patel vs Ahmedabad Municipal Corporation & Another 1985 I LLJ 527 SC*
5. *Mulchandani Electrical and Radio Industries Ltd. vs Workmen 1975 I LLJ 391 SC*
6. *Digwadih Colliery vs Ramji Singh 1964 II LLJ 143 SC*

NATURAL JUSTICE/REASONABLE OPPORTUNITY TO DEFEND/DOMESTIC ENQUIRY, ETC.

1. *Sur Enamel and Stamping Works Ltd. vs Their Workman 1963 II LLJ 367 SC*
2. *Associated Cement Cos. Ltd. vs Their Workmen 1963 II LLJ 396 SC*
3. *Kesoram Cotton Mills Ltd. vs Gangadhar 1963 II LLJ 371 SC*

4. *Khardah & Co. Ltd. vs Its Workmen 1963 II LLJ 452 SC*

5. *Tata Engineering and Locomotive Co. Ltd. vs SC Prasad 1969 (19) FLR 150 SC*

6. *Ananda Bazar Patrika (P) Ltd. vs Their Employees 1963 II LLJ 429 SC*

7. *Employers of Firestone Tyre and Rubber Co. (I) Ltd. vs Their Workman 1967 II LLJ 715 SC*

8. *Tata Oil Mills Co. Ltd. vs Their Workmen 1964 II LLJ 113 SC*

9. *Bata Shoe Co. (I) Ltd. vs D.N. Ganguly 1961 I LLJ 303 SC*

10. *Anil Kumar vs Presiding Officer and Others 1986 I LLJ 101 SC*

11. *The Board of Trustees of the Port of Bombay vs Dilip Kumar R. Nandkarni and Others 1983 I LLJ 1 SC*

12. *Union of India vs Karunakaran Nair 1986 I LLJ 124 Kerala HC*

13. *Arjun Choubey vs Union of India and Others 1984 I LLJ 17 SC*

14. *A.K. Kripak and Others vs Union of India and Others AIR 1970 SC 150*

15. *Nellimerla Jute Mills Co. Ltd. vs Labour Court, Guntur 1981 (59) FJR 315 A.P.H.C*

16. *M/s. India Photographic Co Ltd. vs Saumitra Mohon Kumar 1984 I LLJ 471 Calcutta HC*

17. *Venkataram Sambamurthy vs Union of India and Another 1986 II LLJ 62 Bombay HC*

18. *Pushpa Iyenger vs Indian Airlines and Others 1988 I LLJ 385 Madras HC*

19. *Municipal Corporation of Greater Bombay vs R.D. Tulpule and Others 1979 (54) FJR 372 Bombay HC*

20. *Brooke Bond India (P) Ltd. vs V. Subbaraman (S) and Another 1961 II LLJ 417 SC*

21. *Dunlop Rubber Company (India) Ltd. vs Their Workmen 1965 I LLJ 426 SC*

22. *Jayadevan and Others vs Commandant MSP and Others 1984 I LLJ 521 Kerala HC*

23. *Sreeramulu vs State AIR 1970 114 APHC*

24. *Associated Cement Companies Ltd. vs T.C. Shrivastava and Others 1984 II LLJ 105 SC*

25. *Saran Motors (Pvt.) Ltd. vs Viswanath and Another 1964 II LLJ 139 SC*

26. *M/s. Chembur Cooperative Industrial Estates Ltd. vs M.K. Chatre and Another 1975 II LLJ 357 SC*

27. *Kanhialal vs District Judge and Others AIR 1983 SC 351*

28. *Steel Authority of India Ltd. and Another vs Dilip Kumar Debnath 1989 I LLJ 133 SC*

29. *Workmen of Hindustan Steel Ltd. vs Hindustan Steel Ltd. and Others 1985 I LLJ 267 SC*

30. *Graphite India Ltd. vs State of West Bengal and Others 1980 II LLJ 29 Calcutta HC*

31. *Union of India and Another vs Tulasiram Patel 1985 II LLJ 206 SC*

32. *Managing Director ECIL Hydrabad vs B. Karunakar 1994 I LLJ 162 SC*

33. *Indian Telephone Industries Ltd. vs Devi Shankar Kumar Shukla 2000 I LLJ 531 SC*

34. *J.K. Agarwal vs Haryana Seeds Development Corporation Ltd. 1991 II LLJ 412 SC*

35. *Harinarayan Srivastava vs UCO Bank and Another 1997 II LLJ 620 SC*

36. *Depot Manager, Andhra Pradesh State Road Transport Corporation, Medak vs Md. Ismail and Another 1997 I LLJ 1192 APHC*

37. *Andhra Scientific Co. Ltd. vs Seshagiri Rao and Another 1961 II LLJ 117 SC*

38. *Woodbriar and Sussex Estates Ltd. vs Their Workmen 1960 II LLJ 673 Madras*

39. *Manager of Kisan Degree College vs Sambhu Saran Pandey and Others 1995 II LLJ 625 SC*

40. *Bharat Petroleum Corp. Ltd. Maharastra General Kamgar Union and Others 1999 I LLJ 352 SC*

41. *K.N. Shukla vs Bharat Heavy Electricals Ltd. 1989 I LLJ 374 Delhi HC*

42. *Cipla Ltd. and Others vs Ripu Daman Bhanap & Another 1999 I LLJ 900 SC*

43. *Kalindi (N) & Others vs Tata Engineering and Locomotive Co. Ltd. Jamshedpur 1960 II LLJ 228 SC*

44. *Cescent Dyes and Chemicals Ltd. vs Ram Naresh Tripathy 1993 I LLJ 907 SC*

45. *Md. Shahid vs Aligarh Muslim University and Another 1998 I LLJ 25 SC*

46. *Union of India vs Dinanath Shantaram Karekar and Others 1998 II LLJ 748 SC*

47. *State of U.P. and Another vs T.P. Lal Srivastava 1997 I LLJ 831 SC*

48. *UP (Madhya) Ganna Beej Evam Vikas Nigam Ltd. and Others vs Prem Chandra Gupta and Others 2000 I LLJ 1052 SC*

49. *Tripathy K.L. vs State Bank of India and Others 1984 I LLJ 2 SC*

VICTIMIZATION, UNFAIR LABOUR PRACTICE, PERVERSE FINDING, COMPENSATION IN LIEU OF REINSTATEMENT, ETC.

1. *Hind Construction and Engg. Co. Ltd. vs Their Workmen 1965 I LLJ 462 SC = AIR 1965 SC 917*

2. *Sant Raj and Another vs O.P. Singla and Another 1985 II LLJ 19 SC*

3. *Sudarsan Motors (P) Ltd. vs Ameerjan and Another 1985 II LLJ 22 SC*

4. *Chandulal vs Management of Pan American World Airways Inc. 1985 II LLJ 181 SC*

5. *K.C. Joshi vs Union of India and Others 1985 II LLJ 416 SC*

6. *Bharat Bank Limited, Delhi vs Bharat Bank Employees Union, Delhi AIR 1950 SC 188*

7. *Sengara Singh and Others vs State of Punjab and Others 1984 I LLJ 161 SC*

8. *National Tobacco Co. Ltd. of India and Others vs Fourth Industrial Tribunal and Others 1960 II LLJ 175 Calcutta HC*

9. *Ashok Kumar vs Union of India and Another 1988 II LLJ 344 SC*

10. *Workman of Motor Industries Co. Pvt. Ltd. vs Motor Industries Co. (P) Ltd. 1969 II LLJ 673 SC*

11. *Hamdard Dawakhana Wakf vs Its Workmen 1962 II LLJ 772 SC*

12. *Bengal Bhatdee Coal Co. Ltd. vs Ram Probash Singh and Others 1963 I LLJ 291 SC*

COMPETENT AUTHORITY/DISCIPLINARY AUTHORITY/PUNISHING AUTHORITY

1. *Thobias vs State of Kerala 1987 II LLJ 504 Kerala HC*

2. *Gwalior District Cooperative Bank Ltd. vs Ramesh Chandra Mangal and Others 1985 I LLJ 523 SC*

3. *Rajamani vs State of Tamil Nadu and Others 1986 I LLJ 244 Madras HC*

4. *Steel Authority of India Ltd. Successor of Bokaro Steel Ltd. vs Labour Court and Another 1980 II LLJ 456 SC*

5. *Municipal Corporation of Delhi vs Ram Pratap Singh 1977 I LLJ 303 SC*

6. *D.J. Warkari vs K.V. Karanjikar 1980 II LLJ 270 Bombay HC*

7. *State of Rajasthan vs .M.C. Saxena 1998 I LLJ 1244 SC*

8. *Bank of India and Another vs Degala Suryanarayana 1999 II LLJ 682 SC*

9. *Punjab National Bank vs Kunj Bihari Mishra and Another 1998 II LLJ 809 SC*

10. *State of Madhya Pradesh vs Shardul Singh (1970) I SCC 108: 1971 LAB IC (N) 5*

11. *P.V. Srinivasa Sastry vs Comptroller and Auditor General (1993) I SCC 419: (1993 AIR SCW 550)*

12. *Transport Commissioner, Madras vs A. Radha Krishna Moorthy (1995) I SCC 332: (1995 AIRSCW 1555)*

13. *Inspector General of Police and Another vs Thavasiappan (AIR 1996 Supreme Court 1318)*

DISCHARGE SIMPLICITER/TERMINATION OF SERVICE ETC.

1. *L. Michael & Another vs M/s. Johnson Pumps Ltd. 1975 I LLJ 262 SC*

2. *O.P. Bhandari vs India Tourism Development Corporation and Others 1986 II LLJ 509 SC*

3. *Central Inland Water Transport Corporation and Another vs Tarun Kanti Sengupta, Brojo Nath Ganguly and Others 1986 II LLJ 171 SC*

4. *West Bengal State Electricity Board & Others vs Desh Bandhu Ghosh and Others 1985 I LLJ 373 SC*

5. *Workmen of Hindustan Steel Ltd. and Another vs Hindustan Steel Ltd. 1985 I LLJ 285 SC*

6. *S.R. Tewari vs District Board, Agra 1964 I LLJ 1 SC*

7. *Vidya Ram Mishra vs Managing Committee, Sri Jai Narain College 1972 I LLJ 442 SC*

8. *Union of India and Another vs Tulasiram Patel 1985 II LLJ 206 SC*

9. *Delhi Transport Corporation vs DTC Mazdoor Congress 1991 I LLJ 395 SC*

10. *Uptron India Ltd. vs Shammi Bhan and Another 1998 I LLJ 1165 SC*

11. *D.K. Yadav vs JMA Industries Ltd. 1993 II LLJ 696 SC*

12. *V.P. Ahuja vs State of Punjab and Others 2000 I LLJ 1099 SC*

13. *Dipti Prakash Banerjee vs Satyendra Nath Bose National Centre for Basic Sciences, Calcutta & Others 1999 I LLJ 1054 SC*

14. *Agra Electric Supply Co. vs Alladin 1969 II LLJ 540 SC*

15. *Management of Express Newpapers (P) Ltd. vs Presiding Officer, Labour Court, Madurai, AIR 1964 SC 806*

16. *Brooke Bond India (P) Ltd. vs Y.K. Gautam 1973 II LLJ 454 SC*

17. *Biswajit Deb Roy vs Indian Overseas Bank and Others 1987 II LLJ 288 CAL. HC*

18. *Mohan Lal vs Bharat Electronics Ltd. 1981 II LLJ 70 SC*

POWERS OF LABOUR COURT ETC.

1. *The Workmen of M/s. Firestone Tyre & Rubber Co. of India (Pvt.) Ltd. vs Their Management and Others 1973 I LLJ 278 SC*

2. *Jaswant Singh vs PEPSU Roadways Transport Corp. & Another 1984 I LLJ 33 SC*

3. *M.S. Dantwal vs Hindustan Motors Ltd. and Others 1976 II LLJ 259 SC*

4. *Indian Iron and Steel Co. Ltd. and Another vs Its Workmen 1958 I LLJ 260 SC*

5. *Indian Farmer's Fertilizer Corporation Ltd. etc. vs Presiding officer, Labour Court, Chandigarh 1999 I LLJ 1040 SC*

6. *U.P. State Road Transport Corporation vs Subhas Chandra and Others 2000 I LLJ 1117 SC*

7. *Cooper Engineering Ltd. vs P.P. Mundhe 1975 II LLJ 579 SC*

8. *Shanker Chakraborty vs Britannia Biscuit Co. Ltd. (1979) 3 SCC 371 SC*
9. *Delhi Cloth & General Mills Ltd. vs Ludh Budh Singh 1972 I LLJ 180 SC*

SUSPENSION PENDING ENQUIRY/PRELIMINARY ENQUIRY ETC.

1. *Laxmi Devi Sugar Mills vs Ram Swaroop & Others 1957 I LLJ 17 SC*
2. *Hotel Imperial, New Delhi vs Hotel Workers Union 1959 II LLJ 544 SC*
3. *Balvantrai Ratilal vs State of Maharastra 1968 II LLJ 700 SC*
4. *W.S. Dhamankar vs Cantonment Board, Belgaum 1985 II LLJ 485, Karnataka HC*
5. *T. Kajee vs U. Jormanik Siem 1961 I LLJ 652 SC*

TIME LIMIT FOR RAISING INDUSTRIAL DISPUTE

1. *Ajaib Singh vs Sirhind Co-op Marketing cum Processing Service Society Ltd. & Another 1999 I LLJ 1260 SC*
2. *Mahavir Singh vs UP State Electricity Board and Others 1999 II LLJ 482 SC*
3. *Gurmail Singh vs Principal, Govt. College of Education and Others 2000 I LLJ 1080 SC*
4. *State Bank of Indore vs Govindrao 1997 I LLJ 841 SC*

PARALLEL DOMESTIC ENQUIRY AND CRIMINAL TRIAL

1. *Delhi Cloth and General Mills Ltd. vs Kushal Bhan 1960 I LLJ 520 SC*
2. *Jang Bahadur Singh vs Baijnath Tewari 1969 I LLJ 597 SC*

3. *Kusheswar Dubey vs Bharat Coking Coal Ltd. & Others 1988 II LLJ 470 SC*

4. *T.V. Gauda vs State of Mysore 1975 II LLJ 513 Karnataka HC*

5. *Corporation of Nagpur vs R.G. Modak AIR 1984 SC 626*

6. *Tata Oil Mills Co. Ltd. vs Their Workmen 1964 II LLJ 113 SC*

7. *P.J. Sundararajan and Another vs Unit Trust of India and Another 1993 I LLJ 65 SC*

8. *Depot Manager APSRTC vs Md. Yunif Mia etc. 1997 II LLJ 902 SC*

9. *State of Rajasthan vs B.K. Meena and Others 1997 I LLJ 746 SC*

10. *Captain M. Paul Anthony vs Bharat Gold Mines Ltd. and Another 1999 I LLJ 1094 SC*

11. *Senior Superintendent of Post Office Palthanamthitta vs A. Gopalan 1999 I LLJ 1313*

APPLICABILITY OF EVIDENCE ACT, 1872

1. *Union of India vs T.R. Varma 1958 II LLJ 259 SC*
2. *Central Bank of India vs Prakash Chandra Jain 1969 II LLJ 377 SC*

SOLITARY WITNESS

1. *Banaras Electric Light and Power Co. Ltd. vs Labour Court II Lucknow and Others 1972 II LLJ 328 SC*

RESIGNATION/APPLICATION FOR VRS AND ITS WITHDRAWAL DURING NOTICE PERIOD

1. *Punjab National Bank vs P.K. Mittal 1989 I LLJ 368 SC*
2. *Union of India vs Gopal Chandra Mishra AIR 1978 SC 694*

3. *P. Nagraju vs State of Karnataka and Others 1985 II LLJ 96 Karnataka HC*
4. *Balram Gupta vs Union of India 1987 II LLJ 541 SC*
5. *J.N. Srivastava vs Union of India 1999 I LLJ 546 SC*
6. *Shambu Murari Sinha vs Project Development India and Another 2000 II LLJ 935 SC*

POWERS OF CIVIL COURT TO INTERFERE

1. *Sirsi Municipality by its President, Sirsi vs C.F. Tellis 1973 I LLJ 226 SC*
2. *Executive Committee, UP State Warehousing Corporation Ltd. vs Chandra Kiron Tyagi 1970 I LLJ 32 SC*
3. *Indian Airlines Corporation vs Sukhdev Rai 1971 I LLJ 496 SC*
4 *Premier Automobiles Ltd. vs K.S. Wadke and Others 1975 II LLJ 445 SC*
5. *Sitaram Kashiram Konda vs Pigment Cakes and Chemical Manufacturing Co. 1979 II LLJ 444 SC*
6. *Jitendra Nath Biswas vs Empire of India and Ceylon Tea Co. & Another 1989 I LLJ 572 SC*
7. *Rajasthan State Road Transport Corp. & Another vs Krishnakant 1995 II LLJ 728 SC*

SEC. 17–B "FULL WAGES LAST DRAWN"

1. *Carona Sahu Company Ltd. vs Abdul Karim Muna Khan and Others 1994 I LLJ 1100 Bombay HC*
2. *Hindustan Wires Ltd. vs Janardan Kundu 1998 I LLJ 542 CAL. HC*
3. *Visweswarya Iron & Steel Co. Ltd. vs M. Chandrappa and Another 1993 II LLJ 198 KAR. HC*
4. *Dena Bank vs Kiriti Kr. T. Patel 1998 I LLJ 1 SC*
5. *Rajaram Maize Products vs Brij Lal and Another 1999 II LLJ 799 SC*

NOTATIONS

LLJ = Labour Law Journal
AIR = All India Reporter
FLR = Factory Labour Reports
FJR = Factory Journal Reports
SCLJ = Supreme Court Labour Judgements
SCC = Supreme Court Cases
SC   = Supreme Court
HC   = High Court

Index

About the Author

Dr. G.P. Das Gupta is presently a consultant (HRM) with the Tata group of companies and is based in Jamshedpur. He joined the Tata Iron and Steel Company (TISCO) in 1966 as a Personnel Officer and retired from that company in 2001 as Controller of Establishment. A Ph.D. from the Indian Institute of Technology, Kharagpur, Dr. Das Gupta also holds an MBA from XLRI, Jamshedpur, in addition to a Bachelor of Law degree and Masters' degrees in Economics and Labour & Social Welfare.

Dr. Das Gupta has been associated with XLRI, Jamshedpur, as a faculty member in the PM & IR area for several years. He has previously authored two books—*Handbook on Disciplinary Proceedings* and *Industrial Discipline: Concepts, Laws and Cases*, and also has to his credit numerous articles on topics such as collective bargaining, manpower planning, participative management, industrial relations, and disciplinary proceedings.